VLADIMÍR MUCHA

THE SLOVAK PARADISE

COMPILED BY: DANIEL KOLLÁR

The Slovak Paradise (Slovenský raj)
1ˢᵗ edition, 2001

Editors: Peter Augustini and Daniel Kollár
Hiking tours: Vladimír Mucha
Natural settings: Ján Lacika
Natural landmarks and points of interests: Ján Lacika
Responsible editor: Daniel Kollár
Technical editor: Tibor Kollár
Translation: HACON
Photographs: Ladislav Jiroušek
Attitude profiles: Ján Lacika
Cartography: © Vojenský kartografický ústav, š. p., Harmanec, 2001
Cover: Ján Hladík
Design and layout: Jagus DTP
Print: Kníhtlačiareň Svornosť, a.s., Bratislava

© GEOINFO Slovakia, Ľubľanská 2, 831 02 Bratislava
© DAJAMA, Klimkovičova 1, 841 01 Bratislava
ISBN 80–88975–28–X

Dear readers,

The purpose of the DAJAMA publishers since the beginning of its existence is to promote the regions of Slovakia publishing guidebooks to its geographical and historical assets. Within the series **Regions without frontiers** the individual boundary areas were presented and the series Visiting Slovakia introduced the potential reader to the history and present of the natural historic regions. All books are prepared not only in the Slovak language but also in several foreign languages. Precisely the translations of our guidebooks represent the principal aim of our activities based in the idea to make the attractiveness of Slovakia accessible also to tourists coming from abroad.

The new series **Knapsacked Travel in Slovakia** has been prepared with similar intention. Four books will be published in this series in 2001: The West Tatras (Západné Tatry), The Low Tatras (Nízke Tatry), The Slovak Paradise (Slovenský raj), and The High Tatras (Vysoké Tatry) in four languages: Slovak, English, German, and Polish. As the title of the series suggests, the guidebooks are intended for hikers above all. They contain descriptions of tours, maps illustrating the routes, altitude profiles, classification by exactness and time schedules complemented by photographs of the typical sceneries in most cases. Introduction to the individual books also contains general information, basic characteristics of natural setting of the area in question, and a map of the region with indicated situation of the individual tours. The guidebook also highlights natural landmarks and special points of interests, options to trips, practical information and a register of the most important hiking points.

All recommended tours were written leaning on personal experience of the authors and collaborators. In spite of it, minor changes and discrepancies are possible. We apologize for them and will be grateful if you let us know of any such discrepancy that you may detect. We shall use the information in future editions.

Dear readers,

We are sincerely convinced that you will choose the ideal trip for you from our offer of routes in the most beautiful mountain ranges of Slovakia and will have good time in the romantic setting of the Slovak mountains. We wish you good weather, high spirit and, of course, happy home-coming.

Peter Augustini and Daniel Kollár

Contents

How to use the guidebook

The series Knapsacked Travel in Slovakia is intended for hikers. The introductory part of the book is dedicated to general information on how to plan the individual trips and the basic principles of movement in nature. The first chapter briefly characterizes the natural conditions (starting with surface forms over the waters, climate, soils, vegetation and wild life, ending by the conservation aspect) of the territory in question. A map of the region in scale 1:500 000, which contains the numbered described hiking routes follows.

Then comes the detailed description of the individual routes. A list of the most important information arranged in entries opens each route description. The first entry is the situation of the territory of the route. The second entry is the starting point with the name of the place where the trip starts and the way how to get there (bus stop of SAD = Slovak Bus Transports or the station of ŽSR which means the Railways of the Slovak Republic, a parking lot). The third entry is the finishing point of the route, the place, where the trip ends and the way how to get from there (again bus stop, railway station or parking lot). The fourth entry contains the schedule and the list of the points of the route accompanied by the time that an average hiker needs get to the next point (the time used for relaxing or sightseeing is not included). The fifth entry is information on altitude difference, i.e. the difference between the lowest and the highest points of the trip. The last entry recommends the map of territory of interest, the hiker should have at hand. They are normally available in the local bookstores or newspaper stalls.

Classification of the tour as to degree of difficulty and description of the basic tour follows. The description emphasizes the landmarks. Part of each route is the cutting of map with outlined course of the tour. Medium demanding and demanding routes are also characterised by the altitude profile while the information is complemented by a photograph illustrating the typical setting. Basic routes are compiled in a way, which includes all important areas of the territory. However, the routes are in no way definite. They are rather recommendations, which can be modified or combined (if you overnight in a mountain hotel, for instance) or shortened. Some trips also contain options.

Classification of trips

The proposed routes run normally on well-marked hiking paths and roads. The hiker is always warned of possible orientation trouble. It means increased attention and frequent use of map. All kinds of hikers — from the experienced and fit ones to the inexperienced and comfort-preferring ones — can choose from our offer. The colour of the route numbers, green, blue or red, express three degrees of the trips: little demanding, moderately demanding and demanding routes.

Easy routes are marked in green and they are suitable for older people, families with children and less fit tourists. They are mostly half-day outings running on good roads or paths with low altitude difference and rather short. Medium demanding tours are marked in blue. They are intended for fit hikers and families with grown-up children. They are longer and the altitude difference is higher. Some of them also require orientation sense and some experience with movement in nature. The red-marked tours are for the above-average hikers in excellent physical condition who are used to all-day walk, high altitude difference, use of climbing aids and difficult orientation, and who possess sufficient experience in movement in difficult terrain.

Outfit

The tours in mountain and high-mountain environment always require an adequate outfit and equipment, suitable clothes and footwear including. Plimsolls or low shoes do not protect against injuries in rocky terrain, especially not on moving debris. Also suitable underwear (special thermo-underwear) is important and the upper Polar garments of different thickness are ideal for unstable weather only too frequent in mountains. Weather-proof jackets and trousers (preferably Goratex made) as the top outfit is recommended as well. You will certainly need a plastic mack, cap, mittens, thermo-isolating foil for emergency situations, and the basic medical kit on long and demanding tours. Ski poles and climbing irons even hatchet are recommended if there are snow fields on the route. You should also carry your ID, a watch, map and guidebook, sufficient food and drinks and a disposal bag (to carry the offal back, do not leave it there). Warm clothes are recommended even in hot summer months as the sudden change of weather can be very unpleasant for a hiker lacking the adequate outfit.

Ten basic principles for safe stay in the mountains

1. Chose the tour fitting your possibilities.
2. Inquire about the chosen tour and its state at the nearest Mountain Rescue Service station.
3. Let your host (person in charge of the establishment where you are accommodated) know about the aim of the tour and expected time of return, and write it in the book of trips before you leave.
4. If you are going away for a longer trip always start in the morning.
5. Your footwear should be solid even in sunny weather.
6. Always have waterproof garments at hand.
7. You should go back if the weather starts to deteriorate.
8. Always stick to the marked trail, do not venture into unknown parts and do not step on snow fields.
9. If the trail above the upper timber line is covered by snow and there are not marking poles in sight, it is considered not marked and you must not continue on it.
10. If you cannot return to the place where you are accommodated, you should notify your host.

Ten basic principles of safe hiking

1. Study the map of your the trip and read the guidebook in advance.
2. Always concentrate on the key points of the routes, especially the cross-roads.
3. Abrupt changes of direction or turnings onto less important communications are indicated by a sign (arrow).
4. If you do not find marking in the course of say 300 m where there are enough objects suitable for placing a mark, you have probably gone astray. In that case it is better to go back to the nearest crossroads and find the correct direction.
5. If you are passing through wide open area with hardly discernible paths, please pay attention to the opposite side edge of canopy in case there is a big belt-shaped marking (so-called "tout")
6. There are cases when the rules of marking or the prescribed 3-year interval of renovation of marking were not observed. It can cause poor legibility, insufficient frequency or discrepancy of the marking with regards to the map.
7. Look back from time to time and observe the marking running in the opposite direction. It may be more reliable.
8. It is recommendable to measure the distance quoted in the map if you want to calculate the time of the trip and its length.
9. The data on road posts contain information on distances (the first line of the chart quotes the nearest point with road post on the trail, the second and third line inform about important places on the route and the last line quotes the end point).

Kláštorisko

10. The marked hiking trails are fully utilizable only if there is no snow cover.

Maps

Every route is accompanied by a map with the course of the route. In spite of it, it is recommendable to carry a detailed map issued by VKÚ (The Military Cartographic Institute) Harmanec. Particularly, we recommend the series of maps at scale 1:25 000: No. 1 Nízke Tatry — rekreačné strediská, No. 2 Vysoké Tatry — Starý Smokovec, No. 3 Západné Tatry — Podbanské — Zverovka, No. 4 Slovenský raj, No. 6 Donovaly — Šachtička — Turecká, and No. 7 Pieniny.

Transport

The area of the northern Slovakia boasts comparatively thick network of bus lines and in some cases also railway lines. The starting and finishing points of the individual routes are accessible by the collective means of transport. It means that each tour (with the exception of the trips starting and ending at high-mountain cottages or hotels) can be accomplished by going to its starting point by bus or train.

Prielom Hornádu canyon

Situation

The Slovenský raj Mts. spread between the 48° 50' and 48° 58' of the northern latitude and 20° 10' and 20° 32' of eastern longitude. They are situated in the north of the Slovenské rudohorie mountain range and along with the Muránska planina plateau form part of the Spišsko-gemerský karst. They are 200 to 400 metres taller than the Hornádska kotlina basin, with central and western parts of which it borders in the north. West of the Slovenský raj Mts. are the Nízke Tatry Mts., which are in turn much taller than our area of interest. For instance, the Kráľova hoľa mountain, (1,948 m), which is quite near, is taller than the tallest mountains of the Slovenský raj Mts. by as much as 700 m. The south-eastern border line is less distinct and it separates the Slovenský raj from the Havranie vrchy Mts. The south-western limit is a point of contact with several relief-forming units. The Slovenský raj Mts. are connected with the Muránska planina plateau there. The limit forms here a narrow belt finishing in the north-west by the easternmost protuberance of the Horehronské podolie valley. The Slovenský raj

Biely potok gorge

Mts. have always been a natural border between the historic provinces of Spiš and Gemer. Today they are part of the Košice province. Small parts of our territory though are under the administration of the province of Prešov (district of Poprad) and the province of Banská Bystrica (district of Brezno).

Natural setting

Substratum and surface

The geological building of the territory of the Slovenský raj Mts. is comparatively complicated. The major part of the territory is built by two basic structures. The smaller, western one is the Bebrava unit separated from the eastern larger Northern Gemerit unit by the Muráň fault. Both of them are comparatively homogeneous, as the Mesozoic sedimentary rocks such as dolomite and sandstone prevail in it. As they are built by carbonate rock prone to karstification, the character of the Slovenský raj Mts. is that of a karstic plateau. On the south-eastern edge of this territory older non-karstic rocks formed in the older Palaeozoic Age emerge. Sandstone, quartzite and phyllite rocks are visible in its surface. In the west of the Slovenský raj Mts. crystalline shales and granitoids building the adjacent Kráľovohorské Tatry Mts. appear. The geologically youngest part of the Slovenský raj Mts. is its northernmost area partially covered by the structural unit of the contiguous Hornádska kotlina basin. The Mesozoic rocks

The twelve tallest mountains of the Slovenský raj Mts.		*(in metres)*	
Ondrejisko	1,270.6	Havrania skala	1,153.5
Strmá prť	1,197.8	Kóta nad Priehybou	1,150.3
Kóta n. Vyšnou záhradou	1,197.2	Duča	1,141.7
Javorina	1,185.6	Vahan	1,138.7
Honzovské	1,171.9	Cigánka	1,137.4
Remiaška	1,167.6	Kopanec	1,132.0

covered by the sediments were originally deposited here in the Old Tertiary Sea. The geologists identify them as the Inner Carpathian Flysch, with alternating sandstone and claystone layers lying on the basal group of strata consisting of limestone conglomerates.

The properties of the base rock and tectonic regime of the territory determine the present geomorphic character of the Slovenský raj Mts. in early stages of its development. The comparatively flat and rather short mountains of the Slovenský raj were uplifted in the Tertiary and Quaternary Ages, which caused that the local river network eroded and created narrow and deep valleys. Tectonic movements are responsible for the fact that Slovenský raj Mts. are now in higher position compared to the adjacent Hornádska kotlina basin and in lower position compared with

Klástorská roklina gorge

the high mountain massif of Kráľova hoľa, Stolica Mts., and partially also with Volovské vrchy Mts. The plain-like relief inside the Slovenský raj Mts. is ascending towards the south as a result of asymmetric uplifting of the range. The summits surrounding the Prielom Hornádu canyon reach the altitude 700 to 800 metres above sea level, the high plains further in south are more than 1,000 m high. The tallest mountains are in the south-west including the tallest mountain of the Slovenský raj Mts., Ondrejisko (1,271 m).

Dissection of the Slovenský raj as the result of tectonic uplifting of the massif proceeded depending on the capacity of the rocks to resist the destructive force of the waters of the rivers and torrents. Limestone, the most frequent rock on the surface, resisted for a comparatively long time, but it still contains numerous bizarre rock forms. The interior of the limestone massifs is full of hollows. The water penetrating into the ground created complicated cave systems. The largest of them originated in the south of the Slovenský raj Mts. in the entrails of the Duč Mountain below the high plain of Hanesová. It was discovered on 28th October 1974 and called **Stratenská jaskyňa cave** by the explorers from Spišská Nová Ves. Its exploration took many years. During the first six of them 10,500 m of cave corridors were surveyed. But it did not finished there. Every descent to the dark underground meant more explored meters of corridors. In the 1980´s the Stratenská jaskyňa cave with its 15 km became the longest in Slovakia and remained so until a pass between the caves of Sloboda and the adjacent Mier was discovered in the Demänovská dolina valley. At present the length of the explored cave corridors of the system of the Stratenská jaskyňa cave and Psie diery cave is 21,737 metres and it is the second largest in Slovakia. However, it is not accessible to the public and its wonderful drip-stone ornamentation including some precious aragonite forms, as well as unusually spacious cave corridors and huge halls remain unknown to the tourists. The Rozprávkový dóm (The Dome of Fairy Tales) for instance, is the largest natural underground hall in Slovakia. Its total volume is 79,017 cubic metres, its length is 192 m, mean width is 46 m and it is 11 m high. The stable temperature inside the cave moves around 6 degrees Celsius. The pride of this inaccessible cave is white-coloured drip stone calcite ornamentation, which is in places indeed enormous. It also contains precious hemispheric "pearls". The Lake of Stalagmites, the area of which is 356 square metres dominates among the numerous underground lakes.

In the south-western edge of the Slovenský raj Mts. is the **Dobšinská ľadová jaskyňa cave**, one of the largest ice caves in Europe. It contains 110,132 cubic metres of ice, which is in places up to 25 metres thick. The ice ornamentation of the cave survives thanks to the fact that the shape of the cave is similar to that of a bag with only one opening. It originated some time at the end of the Tertiary Age, approximately simultaneously with the adjacent Stratenská jaskyňa cave separated by the collapse of the connecting corridor. The entrance into the Dobšinská ľadová jaskyňa cave is in the highest part of the 80 metre deep underground space. Cold air flows into the cave in winter and pushes the lighter warm air out of its lower parts. The temperatures in the Malá sieň (Small Hall) drops as low as minus 5 degrees Celsius. The heavier cold air remains in the lower parts of the cave also in summer. The temperature slightly rises only in the upper parts of the cave due to the limited air circulation. The summer temperature in Malá sieň rises to freezing point, which is enough to conserve the ice filling of the cave for ages. The ice, however, is very sensitive to microclimatic changes brought in by the movement of the tourists. Its protection called for a system of measures, such as regulation of visits and installation of special cold lights. The unique Dobšinská ľadová jaskyňa requires constant observation by the experts in meteorology and speleology, the science dealing with caves.

Skating in summer

The mining engineer Eugen Ruffini with two companions Gustáv Lang and Ondrej Még were the first persons, who descended for the first time into an unusual cave filled with ice by the beginning of summer 1870. The discovery of the three brave natives of Dobšiná won an extraordinary response of the public. A great ceremony connected with summer skating was held after two

The environs of Stratená

months. In June of the following year the cave was open to the public and 292 persons visited it before the end of the year. Twelve years after the pioneer exploration inside the Duč Mountain the cave had its electric lighting installed. Dobšinská ľadová jaskyňa cave became the first in the world to have this achievement of modern civilization.

There are more cave systems in the Slovenský raj Mts. apart from Stratenská and Dobšinská ľadová jaskyňa caves. The Medvedia jaskyňa cave is unusually rich in remnants of bodies of now extinct cave bears. More than 15 thousand year old bones of several-weeks old bears and huge adult males weighing 400 kilograms were probably brought here by the water of underground brook, which also modelled hundreds of meters of cave corridors. The speleologists explored so far 487 m of it. The Medvedia jaskyňa cave boasts rich drip-stone ornamentation. The 537 m long Zlatá diera cave possesses an important karst spring the same as the Dlhá jaskyňa cave in Malý Sokol. The water from the Glac plateau irrigates both caves. Since the time immemorial the people have known the caves in place called Čertova sihoť. They are the Čertova diera, Čertova jaskyňa, and Vtáčia jaskyňa caves. A special type of the underground karst is the Tomášovská jaskyňa cave 276 m long, which originated in limestone Tertiary sandstone. As the

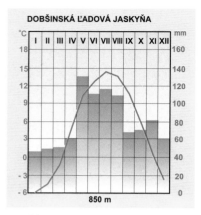

DOBŠINSKÁ ĽADOVÁ JASKYŇA

850 m

Monthly temperatures and precipitation

water quickly got lost in limestone massif, it did not have sufficient time to create a valley network. This is the reason why the high plains survive here. The geographers define them as the remnants of the Tertiary flat relief uplifted by tectonic movement to the height of 500 to 600 meters above the Hornádska kotlina basin. The gorge-like valleys now divide the originally united high plain into several **karstic plateaux**. The largest and best conserved of them is the Glac plateau in the central part of the Slovenský raj Mts. The area of its high plain is more than 3 square kilometres. There are more plateaux there, including the Geravy, Pelc, Hanesová, Skala, and Lipovec. The high plains of the plateaux are slightly undulated with karstic holes and lapies fields. The valleys cutting the plateaux of the Slovenský raj Mts. are extremely narrow, rather gorges then valleys. Fourteen short valleys are shaped as **gorges** and thirteen of them are situated on the northern side of the range in the Hornád basin. Only one of them, the Zejmarská roklina gorge is oriented to the south into the valley of the Hnilec river. Kláštorská roklina gorge ends directly in the The Prielom Hornádu canyon. Suchá Belá ends at the edge of the Slovenský raj Mts. in the valley of the Hornád near Podlesok. Piecky and Veľký Sokol end in the valley of Veľká biela voda. The valley of Tomášovská Belá is the place, where the Sokolia dolina and Kyseľ valleys end. The profile of the gorges in Slovenský raj Mts. is very uneven, with numerous rock steps and the falling water creates cascades there. The altitude difference of the water flowing in gorges is fairly pronounced; it falls in places from the height of as much as 400 metres over the distance of 2.5 kilometres in case of Suchá Belá, for instance. It is supposed that some gorges of Slovenský raj originated by collapse of ceilings of river caves inside the limestone massif.

Some gorges are connected with larger valleys, the nature of which is different, with opened transversal profile. The Veľká Biela dolina valley in the north-west is a large V-shaped one. Similar, but narrower are the Tomašovská Belá valley and the valley of the Lesnica brook in the eastern part of the Slovenský raj Mts. The valley of the **Hnilec river** cuts the southern part of the range. This valley is considered one of the oldest in the Western Carpathians. It presumably originated in the Older Tertiary Age. The stretch of the Hnilec valley, which cuts through the Slovenský raj Mts., has several parts different in shape. It has got a form of bizarre gorge with steep rock faces and a deeply incised valley meander near the village of Stratená. Beyond the gorge the river enters into an area of softer shale rock and the slopes of the valley widen into a smaller intermountain basin, the bottom of which is flooded by the water reservoir of Palcmanská Maša. The valley tapers again near the village of Prostredný Hámor and enters the territory of the contiguous Volovské vrchy Mts.

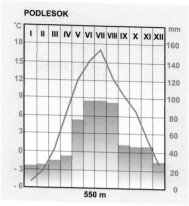

PODLESOK

550 m

Monthly temperatures and precipitation

The end of the Hnilecká dolina valley

The Hnilecká dolina valley, the least age of which is estimated at 50 million years, is "dying". The cause is the altitude difference between the bottom of the upper Hnilec and the adjacent substantially younger valleys. The Hnilec flows now in the bottom of high situated valley, which lies 300 m higher than the bottom of the Dobšinský potok brook. By the way, the local power plant makes use of the altitude difference for production of electricity. Dobšinský potok brook behaves aggressively to its older neighbour in the north and it slowly cuts into the southern slope of the Dobšinský kopec Mt. The dividing crest is gradually pushed towards the Hnilec, the basin of which is gradually diminishing. Similar phenomenon occurs only once in several hundreds of thousand years and its rather poetic name is piracy.

The **Hornád river** in the northern part of the Slovenský raj Mts. has modelled a special **gorge-like valley**. The Flysch sediments covered the entire territory in the Older Tertiary Age. Now they form the contiguous Hornádska kotlina basin. Tectonic movement in time of the Younger Tertiary Age uplifted the Slovenský raj Mts. above the Hornádska kotlina basin. The Hornád responded by deep erosion into the parent rock. It soon reached deeper lying Mesozoic rock. The uplifting was so pronounced that the river did not have time to deviate its stream into the less resistant and softer Tertiary sandstone and conglomerates. It remained restrained in hard limestone and dolomite

Geravy

rocks of the edge of the Slovenský raj Mts. A wonderful canyon known as the Prielom Hornádu canyon with steep rock faces towering above the torrent originated here. It is the most attractive part of the Slovenský raj Mts.

Climate and waters

The Slovenský raj Mts. are situated in the boundary area between the comparatively warm and dry Hornádska kotlina basin and colder and humid Slovenské rudohorie Mountains. This situation determines the climate of the mountains. The most acceptable conditions are in the north of the range, in the territory inclined towards the Hornádska kotlina basin. The environs of Čingov and Podlesok are in moderately warm and moderately humid regions with cold winter, mean July temperature over 16 degrees Celsius and 50 summer days in a year. This territory is within the reach of what is called precipitation shadow of the Tatras, which manifests itself in the Popradská and Hornádska kotlina basins. The average annual rainfall in Podlesok is 648 mm, while the summer months are most rainy and the winter months are the driest. The plateaux and the valley of the Hnilec are colder and more humid. They lie in the moderately cold area of mountain type with mean July temperature 12 to 16 degrees Celsius. The mean annual rainfall of 954

The tallest waterfalls in the Slovenský raj Mts. *(in meters)*

Závojový vodopád (Sokolia dolina)	65
Obrovský vodopád (Kyseľ)	60
Karolínyho vodopád (Kyseľ)	25
Kaplnkový vodopád (Kyseľ)	15
Okienkový vodopád (Suchá Belá)	15
Veľký vodopád (Piecky)	12
Bočný vodopád (Suchá Belá)	12
Terasový vodopád (Piecky)	10
Korytový vodopád (Suchá Belá)	10

mm was taken near Dobšinská ľadová jaskyňa cave. The Kláštorisko and Geravy are colder areas. Central and southern parts of the Slovenský raj Mts. are richer in snow than the drier and warmer north of the range. Podlesok enjoys the mean 78 days of snow cover while Geravy has as much as 118 snow days. Snow cover appears by the beginning of November and lasts until April. Its thickness culminates by 60 to 75 cm in March while it reaches the man value of 26-36 cm in winter. Ski season lasts 3 to 4 months in the Slovenský raj Mts. Western and north-western winds prevail here and the result is pure and dust-free environment, as all large sources of pollution such as those in Rudňany and in Spišská Nová Ves are the localities with less intense air currents. Great micro-climatic differences connected with extreme dissection of the relief in the canyons are typical for the Slovenský raj Mts. In deep and closed valleys the phenomenon called "lakes" of cold and humid air forms because of lack of ventilation. It manifests itself by temperature inversions when the gorges are colder and more humid than the higher situated high plains of the karstic plateaux. Inversions are frequent above all in winter, autumn and in the night.

Water has always been an important component of landscape and it is especially true in case of the Slovenský raj. Water, one of the principal natural elements, flows here in torrents trough deep gorges and canyons, falls over rock thresholds in cascades, and penetrates into the underground of the karstic plateaux to create there wonderful cave systems. From the hydrological point of view Slovenský raj Mts. is a relatively homogeneous territory spreading in the **Hornád basin**. This basin is divided into two parts. Two thirds of the territory of the Slovenský raj Mts. in the north and in the centre are drained by the Hornád while the Hnilec drains the remaining southern third of the territory. The Hnilec is the right side tributary of the Hornád and joins it far from the limit of the Slovenský raj Mts. near Margecany.

The karstic territory of the Slovenský raj Mts. boasts rich supply of **underground water**. The springs in the plateaux are less yielding, they appear in the upper sections of the valleys and irrigate only its immediate environs. Up to now seventeen of them are known. The valley springs are considerably richer in water and 21 are known. A curiosity of the Slovenský raj is what is called the occasional spring next to Havrania skala rock.

Occasional spring

This unique karstic phenomenon has attracted attention of scientists and public more than hundred years ago. As its name suggests that the water of this karstic spring appears in irregular intervals. It is explained by the fact that the spring is connected with the cave system with corridors shaped in form of letter V turned upside down. When the water reaches its top the water falls down the karstic siphon and flows out through a hole in the ground. There used to be an ingenious gadget similar to a little water mill on top of the spring, which made a

Malý Kyseľ

knocking sound every time the water emanated on the surface.

The most important **surface streams** in the Slovenský raj Mts. are the Hornád in the north and the Hnilec in the south. All brooks and torrents flowing through the complicated network of gorges and forested valleys end in these two rivers. Both main rivers leave the territory with comparatively great amount of water. The mean discharge of the Hornád is 6.2 cubic meters per second while the Hnilec is much smaller river with mean discharge of 0.95 cubic metres per second. Their water table rises in spring between March and May in time of snow thaw. The Hornád in its canyon is frozen in winter and tourists use its bed as a track for cross-country ski trips. The waterfalls in the gorges also freeze in winter time and change into beautiful icicles and icefalls.

There are no natural lakes in the Slovenský raj Mts. apart from bowl-shaped depressions filled with water below the gorge waterfalls. In the western edge of the territory is the locality called Hranovnícke pleso lake. In fact there is no water body there. It is a remarkable cascade of **travertine steps,** protected natural phenomenon, where a lake might have existed in the past. Travertine precipitated from water, which emanates from the spring in transversal fault separating the Slovenský raj Mts. from the Low Tatra Mts.

Soil, vegetation and wild life

Carbonate type of soil, especially rendzinas prevail in the karstic Slovenský raj Mts. But also rare relic soil of the *terra calcis* type, locally surviving on the high plains of the karstic plateaux can be found here. It is a very old soil of clay character, which originated in the Quaternary era. Its presence on the high plain below the Malý Kyseľ gave the name to the place Hlinová (hlina means clay in English). Cambisols developed on less carbonate substratum and the rock faces of the gorges are covered by shallow lithosols and rankers.

From the point of view of the phytogeographic division the territory of the Slovenský raj Mts. is classified into the region of the West Carpathian flora with prevailing forest plant associations because 90 percent of the area is covered by forests. The varied nat-

Prielom Hornádu canyon

ural conditions, above all highly dissected terrain and the presence of rich substratum support diversity of vegetation cover. As much as 930 species of vascular plants with 6 endemites linked to the territory of Slovakia live in the Slovenský raj Mts. There are also 19 endemites, which can be found in a wider area, for instance those of the Western Carpathians can be also found here. The Western Carpathian endemites include: *Pulsatilla slavica, Dianthus, Erysimum wittmannii,* and *Festuca tatrae,* while *Campanula carpatica* and *Hesperis nivea* are the Carpathian endemites. Mountain dwarf pine and edelweis are the species rather typical for high-mountain environment but surprisingly enough they also occur in the Slovenský raj Mts. Vegetation of the last glacial is represented in the local flora by several glacial relics such as *Dryas octopetala. Campanula sibirica* and *Carex* grow here near sunny spots on limestone rocks.

Three vegetation steps developed in the territory of the Slovenský raj Mts. The oak-beach step, is the lowest situated, the fir-beach step is the most spread, and the highest situated step consists of spruce-beach-fir forest on the upper parts of the slopes and in cold gorges. The relics of the original pine stands, which survive in the most extreme positions on the rocks, are rare. On the high plains of karstic plateaux one finds comparatively extensive deforested areas covered by meadows and pastures. These are secondary plant associations, which originated when shepherds cleared the forest by burning. These plant associations are very varied due to the nutritious carbonate substratum. The mountain meadows and pastures on the plateaux represent now a valuable component of the landscape of the Slovenský raj Mts. with, beside other, an important aesthetic aspect. Precious small peat associations also deserve attention. The largest peat bog is in the northern part of the Slovenský raj Mts. in administrative territory of the village of Hrabušice. The area of the local peat bog is 57.26 ha. Peat was extracted here until 1983. The locality hosts rare species of *Carex*, *Orchis* and *Typha* or cattail. The river bank vegetation growing along the channel of the Hornád, Hnilec and some larger brooks fulfils an important protective functions.

Zoologists recorded the presence of 4,000 species of invertebrates, including 2,000 species of butterflies, 400 species of bugs and 150 species of molluscs in the Slovenský raj Mts. The vertebrae are represented by 200 species, beside other, by bear, lynx, wolf, wild cat, red deer, marten, and boar. Several species of rapacious and singing birds nest here including redpoll *Acanthis flamea*, thrush *Turdus torquatus*, or nutcracker *Nufraga caryocactes*. Fish living in the torrents is represented by umber *Thymulus thymulus* and chevin *Leucisus cephalus*. There live 165 threatened to critically threatened animal species in the Slovenský raj Mts.

Nature protection
The National park of the Slovenský raj Mts. with its administrative seat in Spišská Nová Ves is one of the youngest national parks in Slovakia. The unusually valuable landscape lying in the boundary area between the two regions of Spiš and Gemer enjoyed the status of a protected landscape area from 1964. This status was changed to National Park in 1988 and the Slovenský raj Mts. occupying an area of 32,744 obtained a higher degree of protection. Approximately one fifth of the National Park is object of even stricter protection in form of 11 national nature reserves and 8 nature reserves. There are also individually protected natural phenomena Novoveská huta, Hranovnícke lake, Dobšinská ľadová cave, and the protected area of Knola. The majority of nature reserves were established in 1964 with the principal aim to protect the most valuable gorges and valleys. The national nature reserve of Kyseľ calls attention with its area of 990 ha. Somewhat smaller national nature reserves Sokol (701 ha) and Stratená (679) protect the gorge-like valley of the Hnilec next to the village bearing the same name.

1 Košiarny briežok and the Medvedia hlava Mt.

Spišská Nová Ves – Košiarny briežok – Medvedia hlava – Kvašné lúky – Spišská Nová Ves

Situation: The Slovenský raj Mts. - North (eastern part).
Starting and finishing point: Spišská Nová Ves, bus stop, railway station, parking lot.
Time schedule: Spišská Nová Ves - Košiarny briežok ¾ h - saddle of Medve-dia hlava 1 h - Medvedia hlava ¼ h - Pod Medveďou hlavou ¼ h - Kvašné lúky 1 ¼ h - Spišská Nová Ves ¾ h.
Total: 4 ¼ hours.
Elevation gain: 433 m.
Map: Slovenský raj 1 : 50 000 (sheet 124), VKÚ, š. p., Harmanec.

Classification: Easy trip, a circle mostly leading on quality roads and footpaths. Only the ascent from the saddle below the Medvedia hlava Mt. to its crest is a bit steep. Short descent to the crossroads below the Medvedia hlava is demanding in terms of orientation, in the consequence of nature calamity. Also the descent through the Kvašné lúky meadows may be somewhat demanding for orientation.
Basic route: The whole route follows the yellow hiking mark through the attractive environment of meadows and forest around the little cottage settlement in the area called Košiarny briežok, which offers opportunity of refreshment.

Start at the railway station of **Spišská Nová Ves** (470 m) and follow the yellow mark (8738) crossing the town in the direction of NS. Ascending turn left before reaching the brickyard along family houses out of the town. Continue on field road on the grassy surface of an airport and gardens. Enter the forest and cross the brook. A moderate ascent through the forest on asphalt road follows until you reach the **Košiarny briežok** crossroads (528 m). Continue on the yellow-marked path ascending on a narrow asphalt road, which runs mostly in the wood up to the saddle of **Medvedia hlava** (815 m). On the right side, north-west of the saddle is inaccessible summit called Matka Božia, which together with Medvedia hlava once formed an independent plateaux. The route abandons asphalt road at the saddle and continues to the left up the forest road, which later changes into a steeper path leading to the crest of the **Medvedia hlava Mt.** (903 m) (no marked path leads to the top of the mountain). Standing on the crest you can enjoy unique views of the Hornádska kotlina basin with the surrounding mountains. There are the Branisko and Čierna hora mountains in the east and the Volovské vrchy Mts. in the south-east. The descent from the crest to the crossroads of **Pod Medveďou hlavou** (865) is steep. It becomes milder following the yellow mark on forest road to the left into undulated terrain. You are passing alternatively through the forest and clearings to the extensive

Kvašné lúky meadows (771 m). Continue on a rather dull field road and later by a water tower descending to the farmyards at the edge of **Spišská Nová Ves**. Turn off the field road to the left onto the footpath running along the state road. Turn to the right later down through the town passing by the Preveza hotel. The route ends at the square with Town Hall. This route is suitable for a cross-country ski trip in winter.

2 Čingov and the Sovia skala rock

Spišské Tomášovce – Ďurkovec – Čingov – Sovia skala – Smižany

Situation: The Slovenský raj Mts. - North (eastern part).
Starting point: Spišské Tomášovce, bus stop, railway station, parking lot.
Finishing point: Smižany, bus stop, railway station, parking lot.
Time schedule: Spišské Tomášovce -

Ďurkovec ½ h - Čingov ¼ h - Sovia skala ½ h - Smižany-Maša ¾ h - Smižany ½ h.
Total: 2 ½ hours.
Elevation gain: 158 m.
Map: Slovenský raj 1 : 50 000 (sheet 124), VKÚ, š. p., Harmanec.

Classification: Easy and comfortable trip on quality roads and paths, clearly marked. Only the ascent to the Sovia skala rock is rather steep. Repeated change of markings requires attention.

Basic route: The tour offers at its beginning a comfortable access to the tourist centre of Čingov in the widened part of the Prielom Hornádu canyon. The first part of the tour is the ascent to the rock terrace of the Sovia skala rock above Čingov and the final part is the walk in the head of the comfortable widened part of the canyon to its end in the Hornádska kotlina basin.

Start at the railway station of **Spišské Tomášovce** (520 m) following the green hiking mark (5723) leading straight through the village to the crossroads of hiking paths. Turn left onto the blue-marked footpath around a

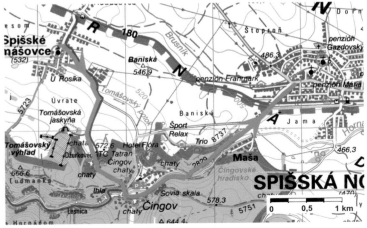

football ground and a farm yard out of the village. Crossing the brook turn to the right up the narrow asphalt road heading to the car camping site in the locality called **Ďurkovec** (565 m). Leaving the crossroads of hiking paths behind stick to the yellow mark (8737) down a forest path to the central orientation point of Čingov (494 m) Continue on the green mark (5751) over the bridge to the right bank of the Hornád river. At the crossroads Čingov-lúka your path leads to the right and up the meadow, between cottages into the forest. The path is steeply ascending to the sightseeing terrace called the **Sovia skala** (640 m). This rock gallery, part of the Čingov Mt., (652 m) offers a beautiful view of the wider part of the Prielom Hornádu canyon with the recreation centre of Čingov. Continue to the right following the blue-marked path (2829). This part of the route contains a comfortable pass through the final part of the Prielom Hornádu gorge, which is skirted by the forested slopes of the Nature Reserve Čingovské hradisko. Finally cross the river to its left bank and ascend from the valley to locality Maša (part of the village of Smižany). The Hornád river abandons here the 16 km long attractive canyon of Prielom Hornádu. Reaching the **Smižany-Maša** crossroads (489 m) continue on asphalt road with blue marking parallel to the yellow marking. Turn right following the blue mark before the underpass and continue along the state road (beware the traffic) to the railway station of **Smižany** (485 m).

Option: You can follow the yellow mark (8737) to the village of Smižany and its bus stop in the final part of the route at the point of the Smižany Maša crossroads, which will take you 15 minutes.

Čingov

3 Around Čingov

Čingov – Lesnica – Bikšová – Košiarny briežok – Sovia skala – Čingov

Situation: The Slovenský raj Mts. -
North (eastern part).
Starting and finishing point: Čingov,
bus stop, parking lot.
Time schedule: Čingov - Lesnica ¼ h -
Bikšová ¾ h - Košiarny briežok ½ h -

Sovia skala 1 h - Čingov ½ h.
Total: 3 hours.
Elevation gain: 146 m.
Map: Slovenský raj 1 : 50 000 (sheet
124), VKÚ, š. p., Harmanec.

Classification: Easy route, a circle in little dissected terrain. Easy orientation thanks to good marking. Only a short descent from the Sovia skala rock
is more demanding.
Basic route: This tour leads in the picturesque terrain of a short stretch of
the Prielom Hornádu canyon and the typical river valley of the Lesnica
brook. It passes through a large mountain meadow of Bikšova lúka, below
the forested slopes of the Matka Božia Mt.
   The route starts in the recreation settlement of **Čingov** (494 m) and the
whole of it is marked in green (5751). Starting at the central orientation point
of Čingov continue to the west for a while, up the stream of the Hornád river.
Cross the bridge to arrive at the **Lesnica** crossroads. This is the point below the
steep limestone faces of the Ludmanka Mt. where you leave the Prielom Hornádu canyon and turn to the left following the green mark. The path moderately
ascends in the valley of the Lesnica brook, mostly in forest. Then you will cross
the narrow wooden footbridge and continue along the brook in the forest about
500 m. Turn left onto forest road and ascend in side valley to the alpine meadow of **Bikšová**. Walk up the meadow as far as the haystack at the saddle. Then
there is a moderate descent down narrow asphalt road along nursery as far as

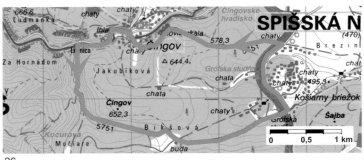

Košiarny briežok

the settlement of **Košiarny briežok** (528 m) situated in the attractive setting amidst meadows and islands of woods. Once you get to the crossroads near gamekeeper's house, continue on the green-marked path around a stall with snacks. Later, during the ascent on the northern edge of the cottage settlement, turn left off the asphalt road and continue between the cottages. The forest road and later path will carry you as far as the sightseeing terrace of the **Sovia skala** rock (640 m) The often visited place offers views of Čingov in the broad part of the Prielom of Hornád canyon, as well as of the part of the Hornádska kotlina basins with the High Tatras in the background. The final stretch of the route is an abrupt descent in the forest to the recreation centre of **Čingov**. This route is also suitable for a cross-country ski trip in winter.

4 Tomášovský výhľad and Kláštorisko

Čingov – Tomášovský výhľad – Letanovský mlyn – Prielom Hornádu – Kláštorská roklina – Kláštorisko – Čertova sihoť – Čingov

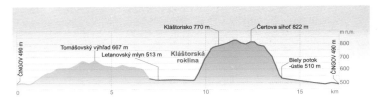

Situation: The Slovenský raj Mts. - North (eastern part).

Starting and finishing point: Čingov, bus stop, parking lot.

Time schedule: Čingov - Ďurkovec ¼ h - Tomášovský výhľad ¾ h - Letanovský mlyn ¾ h - Kláštorská roklina 1 h - Kláštorisko 1 h - Biely potok 1 h - Čingov ½ h.

Total: 5 ¼ hours.

Elevation gain: 280 m.

Map: Slovenský raj 1 : 50 000 (sheet 124), VKÚ, š. p., Harmanec.

Classification: Medium demanding tour in a form of circle. Exposed stretches in the Prielom Hornádu and the Kláštorská roklina gorges secured by footbridges, chains, stairs, and ladders require increased attention.

Basic route: The assets of this route will satisfy any nature lover. It ascends first to the rock gallery called Tomášovský výhľad with superb views. The pass through the central part of the Prielom Hornádu canyon and the ascent

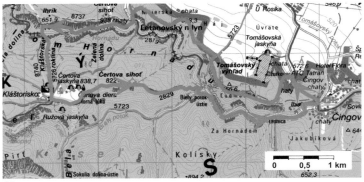

up the tapered gorge of Kláštorská roklina to the grassy plateau of Kláštorisko is also attractive. The pass through the gorge is only allowed in the direction up the stream of the brook.

The route following the yellow mark (8737) continues from the central orientation point at **Čingov** (490 m) on a path heading north-east up between the cottages and later in the forest to the car camping site in the local part called **Ďurkovec** (565 m). Leaving the crossroads behind continue to the left on the yellow-marked path and up the slope of the Ľudmanka Mt. The rock forms called Kazateľnica and Ihla is an ideal spot to pause and enjoy the view of the part of the Prielom of Hornád canyon. The ascent ends on the rock terrace of the **Tomášovský výhľad** (667 m). The rocks are the favourites of the beginning mountaineers and they refer to them as the exercise rocks. Continue comfortably following the yellow path through the forest and later on its edge. At the end of this part is a descent through the forest to forest road and a brook. Turn left where the yellow mark joins the red-marked path (0911) within short distance to the cottages in the locality called the Letanovský mlyn in the wider part of the **Prielom Hornádu** canyon. At the crossroads **Letanovský mlyn** (513 m) turn right in front of the reconstructed Cartesian monastery on the blue-marked trail (2819) heading to the attractive central part of the Prielom Hornádu canyon. Footbridges, chains and stairs secure the demanding pass. Going ahead you will cross the little bridge Nad mlynom and further on a narrow path to another little footbridge called Nad stržou, where you can admire the opposite slope of the Ihrík Mt. The road now descends around the Zelená dolina valley, now closed to the public, and crosses the bridge of Reťazová lávka. The routes continue on a path and steps called Nad Zelenou dolinou. At the head of the valley of Zelená dolina you will find yourself at the entrance to the **Kláštorská roklina** (520 m) gorge. The green mark (5726) carries you further to a demanding ascent up the gorge again secured by chains, steps and ladders. You will gradually pass by the waterfalls called Objaviteľov, Antona Straku, Dúhový vodopád and the cascades of Gusto Nedobrý, Malý vodopád waterfall and the Machový vodopád waterfall. Finally you will ascend with the Kartuziánsky vodopád waterfall on your right to **Kláštorisko** (770), which offers the opportunity to rest and take refreshment or to see the Cartesian monastery. The route continues from Kláštorisko on the blue-marked path (2829) to the east. The first stretch of the path heads upward on the edge of a meadow and later you will descend through the forest on the ridge of the Čertova sihoť with nice views of the environs. At the end of the stretch the path becomes steeper, you will have to make use of the chains fixed in the rocks to get to the crossroads of **Biely potok** (510 m). The route turns to the right following the blue mark across the bridge. Comfortable forest road in the broad part of the Prielom Hornádu canyon will get you as far as **Čingov**, where you will certainly appreciate refreshment at one of the local mountain hotels or cottages.

5 The Prielom Hornádu canyon – east

Čingov – Pod Tomášovským výhľadom – Letanovský mlyn – Kláštorisko – Biely potok – Čingov

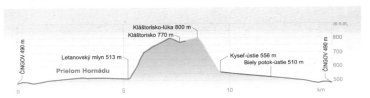

Situation: The Slovenský raj Mts. - North (eastern part).
Starting and finishing point: Čingov, bus stop, parking lot.
Time schedule: Čingov - Biely potok ½ h - Pod Tomášovským výhľadom ¼ h - Letanovský mlyn ¾ h - Kláštorisko 1 h - Kyseľ ½ h - Biely potok ¾ h - Čingov ½ h.
Total: 4 ¼ hours.
Elevation gain: 280 m.
Map: Slovenský raj 1 : 50 000 (sheet 124), VKÚ, š. p., Harmanec.

Classification: Medium difficult tour in a form of circle. Short stretches in the Prielom Hornádu canyon secured by artificial aids are the most exacting. They require increased attention. The ascent to Kláštorisko followed by steep descent to the Biely potok brook, and the short sections in the Tomášovská Belá secured by wooden ladders are also demanding. The rest of the route runs in not demanding terrain. The route is well-marked and orientation is easy. Pay attention to colour of the marking, which changes several times in the course of the route.
Basic route: The tour makes possible to see the attractive eastern area of the Prielom Hornádu canyon, which is part of the National Nature Reserve of Prielom Hornádu. It ascends to the meadow plateau of Kláštorisko. The recreation centre right in the heart of the northern part of Slovakia is the easternmost part of the extensive karstic plateau of Glac. The final stretch is the walk through the picturesque river valley of the Tomášovská Belá secured by little bridges and wooden ladders.

Start at the central orientation point at **Čingov** (490 m) following the blue mark (2829) going west along the stream of the Hornád river, below the rock forms of Kazateľnica, Ihla and Tomášovský výhľad. At the crossroads of **Biely potok-ústie** (510 m) turn right across the bridge where the blue and green marks lead to the following crossroads also called Biely potok (524 m). Advance now following the green mark (5723) across the bridge **Pod Tomášovským výhľadom** to the crossroads. Continue on the blue mark (2819) by attractive though demanding pass through the part of Prielom

Hornádu canyon secured by bridges, chains and steps. Continue crossing the bridge Nad úžinou towards the steps Nad tišinou. Later there are the steps of Pri jaskyni and finally you have to climb the steps Pod mlynom. Leaving the spring behind continue on a comfortable forest road to the **Letanovský mlyn** in the widened part of the Prielom Hornádu canyon. You will finally leave the Prielom Hornádu canyon at the crossroads of the Letanovský mlyn (513 m) in front of the reconstructed Cartesian monastery. Turn right onto the red mark (0911). Ascend up a steeper forest path and later moderately ascending forest road to **Kláštorisko** (770 m), which offers refreshment and sightseeing of the monastery. In the following part of the trip continue from the Kláštorisko crossroads shortly on the yellow path (8886) to the Kláštorisko-lúka crossroads (755 m). Turn right down the yellow mark and walk on the more abruptly descending path into the valley of Tomášovská Belá. Continue left from the crossroads **Kyseľ-ústie** (556 m) following the green mark now. This is a bit demanding stretch secured by bridges and wooden ladders. Walk ahead along the pristine Biely potok brook. Once you get to the **Biely potok-ústie** crossroads continue following the blue mark (2829) back to **Čingov** like at the beginning of the trip.

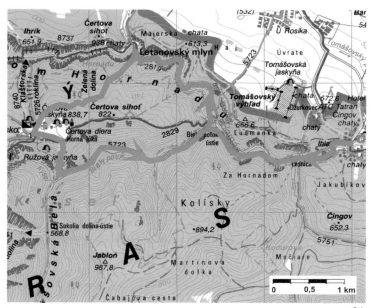

6 The Sokolia dolina gorge

Čingov – Biely potok – Sokolia dolina – Kláštorisko – Čertova sihoť – Čingov

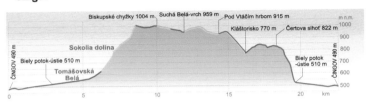

Situation: The Slovenský raj Mts. - North (eastern part).

Starting and finishing point: Čingov, bus stop, parking lot.

Time schedule: Čingov - Biely potok ½ h - Kyseľ ¾ h - Sokolia dolina ½ h - Sokolia dolina 2 h - Biskupské chyžky ¼ h - Glac-Malá poľana ½ h - Suchá Belá ¼ h - Pod Vtáčím hrbom ½ h - Kláštorisko ½ h - Biely potok 1 h - Čingov ½ h.

Total: 7 ¼ hours.

Elevation gain: 514 m.

Map: Slovenský raj 1 : 50 000 (sheet 124), VKÚ, š. p., Harmanec.

Classification: Toilsome and demanding circle for its length (21 km), altitude difference and the ascent up the most exposed gorge of the Sokolia dolina. Ladders, steps, and bridges secure it. It requires precaution. The passage through the gorge is only in one direction, that up the stream of the brook! The passage on the wooden ladders in the Tomášovská Belá valley and a short descent from the Čertova sihoť secured by chains is demanding.

Basic route: Demanding but beautiful tour passing through the Nature Reserves of Prielom Hornádu and Kyseľ canyons. First it leads in little demanding stretch of the Prielom Hornádu canyon to the picturesque river

32

valley of Tomášovská Belá. It leads further through the awe inspiring Sokolia dolina gorge to the karstic plateau of Glac and to recreation centre of Kláštorisko in the heart of the northern part of the Slovenský raj Mts.

Start at **Čingov** (490 m) westward following the blue mark (2829). The comfortable first part of the trip runs in the widened part of the Prielom Hornádu canyon on forest road below the rocks of Kazateľnica, Ihla and Tomášovský výhľad. Continue on the green mark (5723) from the crossroads of **Biely Potok-ústie** (510 m) to the valley of Tomášovská Belá always along the glittering Biely potok brook. Stick to narrow path with wooden ladders and footbridges until you reach the end of the Sokolia dolina valley. At the crossroads of Sokolia dolina-ústie (569 m) turn right up the yellow-marked path (8741) to the **Sokolia dolina** gorge. The first part of the ascent is less demanding as you are proceeding in the wider part of the gorge along the brook and a channel with wooden ladder up beyond the Skalný vodopád waterfall. Steeper ascent follows before you reach the highest waterfall of the Slovenský raj Mts. - the **Závojový vodopád** waterfall. This is the point where the most exposed part of the ascent starts. The rock face of the 70 m high waterfall falling down several rock steps can be climbed with the aid of a system of ladders, chains and two footbridges. You will leave the Závojový vodopád waterfall beyond the second footbridge and continue across the Vyšný vodopád waterfall. The route is then less demanding on a path along the brook and in its final part on steeper forest road heading to the crossroads of the Sokolia dolina-vrchol (1,002 m). Continue to the right following the green mark (5745) and walk comfortably through the forest of the Glacká planina plateau along cottages towards the crossroads called **Biskupské chyžky** (1,004 m).Then descend following the yellow mark in half-open terrain as far as the alpine meadow and the **Glac-Malá poľana** crossroads (992 m). A beautiful view of the Havrania skala rock accompanies you. Continue to the right following the blue mark (2829) and advance later on narrow and short asphalt road to the **Suchá Belá-vrchol** crossroads (959 m). Continue on yellow mark (8890) on forest road and slightly descending you will reach the Pod Vtáčím hrbom crossroads (915 m). Now you are leaving the Glacká cesta road and the next step is the turning right and a comfortable descent on the red-marked path (0911) through the forest to **Kláštorisko** (770 m) with possibility to take some refreshment and see the restored Cartesian monastery. Leave this favourite resting point going eastward on the blue-marked (2829) footpath. The road leads up on the edge of a meadow for a while and then descends down the forested ridge offering fine views. Finally the descent becomes steeper and climbing down with the aid of chains you will find yourself at the crossroads of Biely potok-rázcestie (524 m). Turn right and follow the blue and green marks over a little bridge to the Biely potok-ústie crossroads. Return to **Čingov** on the blue mark like at the beginning of the route. A glass of good beer in one of the hotels will be especially tasty after this difficult tour.

7 The Suchá Belá gorge

Podlesok – Suchá Belá – Kláštorisko – Podlesok

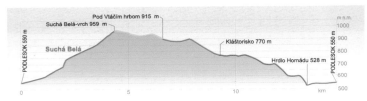

Situation: The Slovenský raj Mts. - North (western part)
Starting and finishing point: Podlesok, bus stop, parking lot.
Time schedule: Podlesok - Suchá Belá 2 h - Pod Vtáčim hrbom ½ h - Kláštorisko ½ h - Pod Kláštoriskom ¼ h - Hrdlo Hornádu ¾ h - Podlesok ¼ h.
Total: 4 ¼ hours.
Elevation gain: 409 m.
Map: Slovenský raj 1 : 50 000 (sheet 124), VKÚ, š. p., Harmanec.

Classification: Medium difficult, comparatively demanding tour in a form of circle. Wooden and iron ladders, chains, steps and footbridges secure exposed stretches in the gorge. They require an extra caution. The passage through the gorges is one-way, up the stream of the brook only. The rest of the route runs on comfortable forest roads and paths. The route is well-marked, pay attention to colour of the markings as they change often.
Basic route: The proposed route offers a fascinating passage through the gorge of Suchá Belá, part of the National Nature Reserve bearing the same name. The demanding passage through the mysterious scenery of cascades, waterfalls and abysses is secured by artificial climbing aids.

Passing by the road post standing in front of the reception of the car camping site **Podlesok** (550 m) on green-marked path you enter directly the **Suchá Belá** gorge. Walk southward on a meadow along the hedge of the camping site. Descend to the channel of the Suchá Belá and a stretch through forest follows. The introductory less demanding section of the Suchá Belá leads alternatively on path and wooden footbridges on the banks and in the channel of the brook as far as the abyss of the Misové vodopády waterfalls. An exposed ascent starts here. Once above the Misové vodopády waterfalls you pass in the channels over the narrowest place called Roklina. Cross the rock window, continue above the Okienkový vodopád waterfall and further on in the widest part toward the Korytový vodopád waterfall. Carry on along the Bočný vodopád waterfall again into the tapered part of the gorge, over the Kaskády. The route beyond them is less demanding as it runs along the brook in the wider part of the gorge. Finally there is a steep ascent through the forest. Passing by a little well you will get onto a narrow asphalt road. Turn left and shortly after you will reach the **Suchá Belá-vrchol** (959 m) crossroads. The ascent ends on the edge of the distinct karstic plateau of Glac. Continue on comfortable forest road and following the yellow mark (8890) descend down to the crossroads **Pod Vtáčím hrbom** (915 m). You will abandon the Glac road at this point and continue to the right on the red-marked path (0911). Proceeding through the forest in the forested part of the Glac plateau you will gradually reach its easternmost point in **Kláštorisko** (770 m). Recreation centre in the heart of the northern part of the Slovenský raj Mts. offers refreshment and sights of the Cartesian monastery, now under reconstruction. Leaving this favourite place of rest continue taking the green-marked path (5726) north-westward. The maintained road will take you across the meadow, then descend through the forest to the **Pod Kláštoriskom** (740 m) crossroads. Turn right

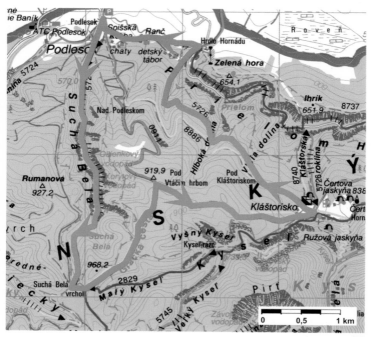

off the forest road onto path. Stick to the green mark and descend in forest by the recreation centre toward the **Hrdlo Hornádu** crossroads (528 m). The confluence of the Veľká Biela voda and the Hornád is the starting stretch of the canyon-like channel of the Hornád. Continue on the blue-marked (2819) path westward along the brook and later on asphalt road as far as **Podlesok**. Some of the local cottages and the car camping site offer opportunity of refreshment and accommodation.

The Misové vodopády waterfalls

8 The Piecky gorge

Podlesok – Píla – Piecky – Pod Vtáčím hrbom – Podlesok

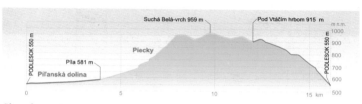

Situation: The Slovenský raj Mts. - North (western part)
Starting and finishing point: Podlesok, bus stop, parking lot.
Time schedule: Podlesok - Píla 1 h - Suchá Belá 2 h - Pod Vtáčím hrbom ½ h - Nad Podleskom ½ h - Podlesok ½ h.
Total: 4 ½ hours.
Elevation gain: 409 m.
Map: Slovenský raj 1 : 50 000 (sheet 124), VKÚ, š. p., Harmanec.

Classification: Medium difficult tour, which is a circle. Exposed stretches in the gorge are secured by artificial climbing aids. They required increased caution. The passage through the gorge is one-way, up the stream of the brook only. The beginning and the end of the route are in comfortable terrain on forest roads and paths. Easy orientation, as the paths are well and visibly marked.

Basic route: The tour will show you one of the two westerly situated gorges of the Slovenský raj Mts. Its first stretch runs in the attractive wide river valley of Veľká Biela voda followed by the stretch in the canyon. The most attractive but also demanding part of the trip is the ascent in the Piecky gorge, within the National Nature Reserve of Piecky. Ladders, steps and chains secure the passage.

The introductory stretch follows the green mark (5724) in little demanding terrain heading to the valley of the Veľká Biela voda brook. Start westward at the camping site of **Podlesok** (550 m) walking along its fence. Later the path enters the forest and leads along the brook. In the short tapering of the valley of Veľká Biela voda the path continues through the canyon-like part called Tiesnina, secured by technical aids. Then advance along the recreation buildings turning to the right upward onto asphalt road and walk as far as the **Píla** settlement (581 m). At the Píla crossroads leave the valley and continue to the left following the yellow mark (8890) leading to the **Piecky** gorge. The path along the brook first ascends mildly in the wide valley of Biela dolina. At its next branching turn left in the direction of the

37

Stredné Piecky. This is where the demanding ascent up the gorge starts. First it is the passage across the Veľký vodopád waterfall. Continue in the channel over the cascades to the next branching of the little valleys. Turn right up across the Tiesňový vodopád waterfall. Ascend in the channel and up the steep slope. Continue to the left by more comfortable traversing road as far as the **Suchá Belá-vrchol** (959 m) crossroads. Continue on the yellow marked trail on the Glacká cesta road running along the edge of the karstic plateau of Glac. This route was a trading road between the regions of Gemer and Spiš in the past. The forest road leads to the crossroads of **Pod Vtáčím hrbom** (915 m). Continue descending down the Glacká cesta road following the red mark (0911) and the comfortable descent along the Nad Podleskom crossroads (700 m) ends at **Podlesok**.

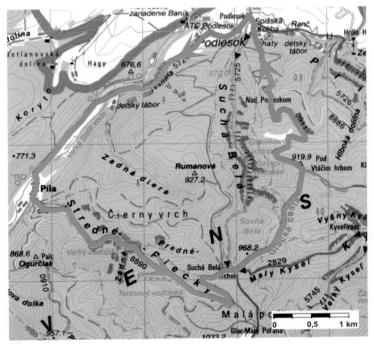

Piecky

9 The Veľký Sokol gorge

Podlesok – Píla – Veľký Sokol – Glac – Pod Vtáčím hrbom – Podlesok

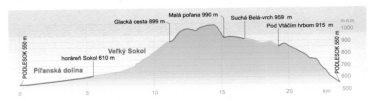

Situation: The Slovenský raj Mts. - North (western part)
Starting and finishing point: Podlesok, bus stop, parking lot.
Time schedule: Podlesok - Píla 1 h - Veľký Sokol ½ h - Glacká cesta 2 ½ h - Glac ¼ h - Malá Poľana ½ h - Suchá Belá ½ h - Pod Vtáčím hrbom ½ h - Podlesok 1 h.
Total: 6 ¾ hours.
Elevation gain: 440 m.
Map: Slovenský raj 1 : 50 000 (sheet 124), VKÚ, š. p., Harmanec.

Classification: A difficult and demanding circle. It is demanding for its length (21 km) and exposed ascent in the gorge secured by ladders, steps, chains and a footbridge. It requires increased caution. It is the one-way ascent, up the brook stream only.
Basic route: It is a very attractive though demanding route. It presents the different nooks of the Slovenský raj Mts. At the beginning it runs in the beautiful wide river valley of the Veľká Biela voda brook. But the difficult stretch of the longest gorge of the Slovenský raj is the most attractive. It leads in ascending terrain over several waterfalls and cascades, parts of the National Nature Reserve of Sokol. The route first follows the green mark (5724) westward and later south-westward to the valley of the Veľká Biela voda brook.

Start at the car camping site at **Podlesok** (550 m), pass by its fence and continue along the brook on forest road. In the short tapering of the valley of Veľká Biela voda walk through the canyon-like part called Tiesnina, secured by technical aids. Continue along the recreation buildings to the right upward onto asphalt road as far as the **Píla** settlement (581 m). Leaving the Píla crossroads behind continue on green-marked path, later field road below the forest as far as gamekeeper's lodge. At the **Veľký Sokol-ústie** crossroads (610 m) turn left and continue following the yellow mark (8772), which leads to the **Veľký Sokol** gorge. Beyond the branching of the valley walk on comfortable forest road along the brook. After about half an hour after the next branching turn left into the channel. This is where the exposed passage through wild gorge starts. Ascend on the banks of the brook and its

40

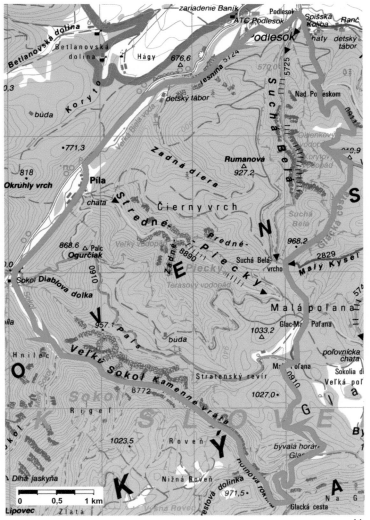

Malý vodopád waterfall

channel to the tapered part over the Kamenné vráta gate in ever steeper terrain, using the climbing aids available. You are passing by several springs over the Malé kaskády and Malý vodopád waterfall. Later the Veľké kaskády and Veľký vodopád waterfall follow. Crossing the footbridge the gorge becomes somewhat wider. Continue in the channel to the final tapering of the gorge, the Rothova roklina ravine. At its end turn left up through the forest to the **Glacká cesta** crossroads (899 m). Continue on the Glacká cesta road to the left following the red mark (0910). The passage through the meadow and forest environment of the Glacká planina plateau is one of the most pleasant parts of this tour. The Glacká cesta road used to be a trade road, which connected the regions of Gemer and Spiš in the past. The ascent

Rothova roklina gorge

in the forest to the edge of the Glac plateau ends on a meadow near the Glac crossroads (former gamekeeper's lodge, 990 m). Follow the red mark walking in forest part of the plateau towards the **Malá poľana-rázcestie** crossroads (990 m). Take the blue-marked path (2829) running in the meadows to the Glac-Malá poľana crossroads (992) where a nice view of the Havrania skala rock opens. Continue on the blue-marked narrow asphalt road trough the forest to the **Suchá Belá-vrchol** crossroads (959 m). Change to the yellow-marked path (8890) and descend still on the Glacká cesta road in the forest to the crossroads **Pod Vtáčím hrbom** (915 m). Turn left onto the red-marked path (0911). The continuous descent leads by the crossroads Nad Podleskom as far as **Podlesok** where you can rest and take refreshment.

10 The Prielom Hornádu canyon – west

Podlesok – Prielom Hornádu – Letanovský mlyn – Ihrík – Zelená hora – Podlesok

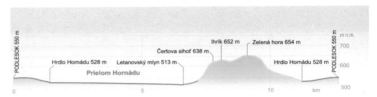

Situation: The Slovenský raj Mts. - North (western part)

Starting and finishing point: Podlesok, bus stop, parking lot.

Time schedule: Podlesok - Hrdlo Hornádu ¼ h - Kláštorská roklina 1 h - Letanovský mlyn 1 h - Hrdlo Hornádu 1 ¼ h - Podlesok ¼ h.

Total: 3 ¾ hours.

Elevation gain: 134 m.

Map: Slovenský raj 1 : 50 000 (sheet 124), VKÚ, š. p., Harmanec.

Classification: Medium difficult circle. The first part of the trip is in exposed canyon-like stretch of the Prielom Hornádu canyon. Footbridges, chains, steps, and ladders secure it. The passage requires special caution. The second part of the trip is in comfortable terrain on forest paths.

Basic route: The tour is an attractive combination of a demanding passage through a part of the Prielom Hornádu canyon and the fairly comfortable passage over the crest of the Ihrik Mt. The greater part of the tour is in the National Nature Reserve of Prielom Hornádu.

The route starts at the car camping site at **Podlesok** (550 m). Follow the blue mark (2819) heading eastward. First it is a narrow asphalt road and

Navigating down the Prielom Hornádu canyon

later it turns left around the Veľká Biela voda brook onto a path. Walk as far as its confluence with the Hornád. The tapered place called Hrdlo Hornádu is the initial part of the passage through the **Prielom Hornádu** canyon secured by artificial climbing aids. Crossing the bridge and having left the **Hrdlo Hornádu** crossroads (528 m) behind turn right following the blue mark on a path along the Hornád. Exposed stretches start beyond a little log hut. Climbing up and using the steps called Pod Zelenou horou and Pri Mníchovej jaskyni, crossing the chain footbridge you will get to the right bank of the Hornád and to the steps called Nad večným dažďom. Continue climbing over the steps of Nad Lanovou lávkou to the **Kláštorská roklina-ústie** crossroads (520 m). Turn left following the blue mark across the Lanová lávka footbridge to the left bank. The path will carry you to the steps called Pri záreze and later to more steps including the Nad Zelenou dolinou. Chain footbridge leads to the right bank of the Hornád. Now you are walking on the river bank upward to the Nad Stržou footbridge. This place offers a fine view of the opposite limestone slope of the Ihrík Mt. Continue downwards and after a while cross the bridge Nad Mlynom to the attractive widened part of the Prielom Hornádu gorge towards the Letanovský mlyn mill. The path leads among the cottages to the crossroads of **Letanovský mlyn** (513 m) near the reconstructed Cartesian stone bridge. Continue following the yellow mark (8737) up the steep forest path as far as the edge of the crest of the **Ihrík Mt.** (652 m). Ascend the crest with rocks called Lievik and Tunel. Then a short ascent to the **Zelená hora Mt.** (654 m) follows. You are leaving the crest and descending in the forest along the remains of the Marcelov hrad castle from the 13th century and a ski lift back to Hrdlo Hornádu. Return to **Podlesok** following the blue mark (2819) like at the beginning of the trip.

45

11 The Kláštorská roklina gorge and Kláštorisko

Podlesok – Hrdlo Hornádu – Prielom Hornádu – Kláštorská roklina – Kláštorisko – Podlesok

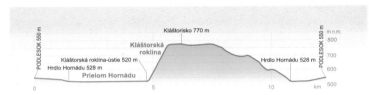

Situation: The Slovenský raj Mts. - North (western part)

Starting and finishing point: Podlesok, bus stop, parking lot.

Time schedule: Podlesok - Hrdlo Hornádu ¼ h - Kláštorská roklina 1 h - Kláš-torisko 1 h - Pod Kláštoriskom ¼ h - Hrdlo Hornádu ¾ h - Podlesok ¼ h.

Total: 3 ½ hours.

Elevation gain: 250 m.

Map: Slovenský raj 1 : 50 000 (sheet 124), VKÚ, š. p., Harmanec.

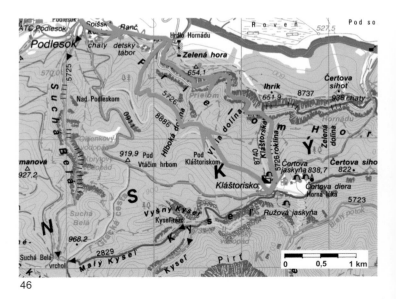

Classification: Medium difficult and demanding circle with exposed stretch in the Prielom Hornádu gorge and in the Kláštorská roklina gorge. Ladders, steps and little footbridges secure these stretches. They require caution. The passage through the gorge is one-way up the stream of the brook only. The rest of the trip runs on the comfortable forest roads and paths. Orientation is easy thanks to good marking.

Basic route: Attractive tour to the often visited and varied landscape in the northern part of the Slovenský raj Mts. The stretch limited by Hrdlo Hornádu and Kláštorisko is in the territory of the National Nature Reserve of Prielom Hornádu. The tour starts by the passage of the western exposed part of the Prielom Hornádu canyon immediately above the river stream. Ascent across several waterfall of the Kláštorská roklina gorge ending in Kláštorisko follows.

The tour starts going eastward from the car camping site at **Podlesok** (550 m) on blue-marked path (2719). Walking on narrow asphalt road turn left on the footpath along the Veľká Biela voda brook as far as its confluence with the Hornád. The rocky tapering called **Hrdlo Hornádu** is the beginning of the passage through the Prielom Hornádu gorge. Beyond the bridge at the crossroads of Hrdlo Hornádu (528 m) turn right onto the path marked in blue running by the river. Exposed stretches secured by climbing aids start beyond the log hut. You are gradually climbing up the steps Pod Zelenou horou and Pri Mníchovej jaskyni. The chain footbridge leads to the right bank of the river and to the steps called Nad Večným Dažďom and Nad Lanovou Lávkou. Leave the Prielom Hornádu gorge at the crossroads of **Kláštorská roklina-ústie** (520 m) and turn right up the path marked in green (5726). The demanding ascent up the Kláštorská roklina gorge is secured by artificial climbing aids. Stick to the brook and walking in its channel gradually climb up the vodopád Objaviteľov waterfall, that of Anton Straka and Dúhový vodopád waterfalls. Then the cascades of Gusto Nedobrý and Malý vodopád waterfall follow. Passing through the Machový vodopád waterfall you will arrive at the more open part of the ravine. In the final part left from the Kartuziánsky vodopád waterfall is only one ascent up the slope, which ends in **Kláštorisko** (770 m). This centre of recreation on a meadow is the easternmost part of the karstic plateau of Glac. It offers the possibilities of refreshment and sightseeing of the Cartesian monastery, now under reconstruction. The trip continues from this favourite stop of tourists in the north-western direction following the green mark. Crossing the meadow continue in undulated terrain in the forest towards the **Pod Kláštoriskom** crossroads (740 m). Turn right off the road onto a path and follow the green mark. A descent through the forest follows. The last stretch of the tour runs along recreation buildings to the Hrdlo Hornádu and the return to **Podlesok** is like at the beginning, sticking to the blue mark (2819).

12 Zejmarská roklina gorge and Čertova hlava

Dedinky – Biele Vody – Zejmarská roklina – Geravy – Predný Hýľ – Čertova hlava – Chotárna dolka – Biele Vody – Dedinky

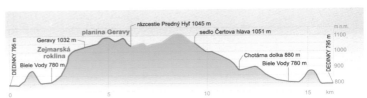

Situation: The Slovenský raj Mts. - South (eastern part)

Starting and finishing point: Dedinky, bus stop, railway station, parking lot.

Time schedule: Dedinky - Biele Vody ½ h - Geravy ¾ h - Predný Hýľ ¾ h - Zadný Hýľ ¼ h - Čertova hlava ½ h - Chotárna dolka ½ h - Biele Vody ½ h - Dedinky ½ h. **Total:** 4 ¼ hours.

Elevation gain: 271 m.

Map: Slovenský raj 1 : 50 000 (sheet 124), VKÚ, š. p., Harmanec.

Classification: Medium difficult circle. Ladders, steps and chains secure the ascent in the short exposed gorge of the Zejmarská roklina gorge. It requires extreme caution. The passage through the gorge is one-way only. The remaining parts of the route are in comfortable terrain on forest roads and paths.

Basic route: The tour runs in the varied landscape of the southern part of the Slovenský raj Mts. The most difficult stretch is the passage through the short romantic gorge of the Zejmarská roklina equipped with technical aids. It is part of the National Nature Reserve bearing the same name. After ascending the edge of the Geravy plateau follows the traverse under the Hýľ to the Čertova hlava saddle with fine views.

The route starts at the village of **Dedinky** (795 m) on red-marked path (0908) heading to the south-east. First you are walking on asphalt road along the water reservoir. When you arrive at the hotel turn left still sticking to the red mark. Pass by the cottage of Horská služba (Mountain Rescue Service) into the forest and walk as far as the foothill of the ski tracks. Walking along the edge of ski track you will get to the settlement of Biele Vody. At the crossroads of **Biele Vody** (780 m) turn left up on the blue-marked path running along the brook. Now you are entering the gorge of **Zejmarská roklina**. Using technical aids climb up the vodopád kpt. Jána Nálepku waterfall. After the demanding passage through the gorge there is a comparatively easy ascent through the forest passing by a spring called Zejmarská studňa as far as the edge of the large karstic plain to the crossroads of **Geravy** (1,032 m). You can buy some refreshment in the building of the top station of chair lift from Dedinky. Continue through the romantic forest and meadow environment of the plateau to its eastern edge. Follow the green mark (5723) in the north-eastern direction on forest road. Now you are walking through meadows to the edge of the plateau, to the crossroads of **Predný Hýľ** (1,045 m). The route continues following the yellow mark (8743) by the crossroads of **Zadný Hýľ** (1,037 m). Then it traverses mostly in the forest while you are walking to the **Čertova hlava** saddle (1,051 m). Turn right there down the red mark (0908). After about 1.5 km you turn right off the road onto the path. Traverse and descend in half-open terrain to the **Chotárna dolka-rázcestie** crossroads (800 m) follows. Continue on the red-marked path, which ascends a bit to open terrain at the saddle called Okrúhla jama with the views of the surrounding landscape. Continue then down the meadows in the direction of the village of **Biele Vody**. Return to **Dedinky** the same way as at the beginning, following the red mark.

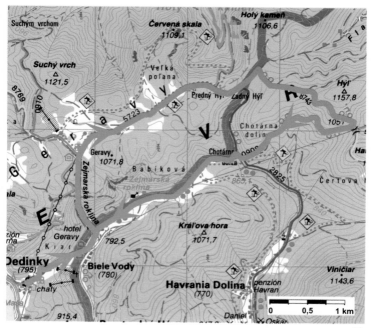

13 The Geravy plateau and Havrania skala

Dedinky – Geravy – Malý Zajf – Občasný prameň – Havrania skala – Stratená – Dedinky

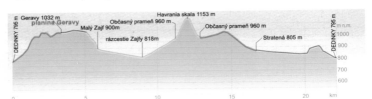

Situation: The Slovenský raj Mts. - South (eastern part)
Starting and finishing point: Dedinky, bus stop, railway station, parking lot.
Time schedule: Dedinky - Geravy ¾ h - Malý Zajf ½ h - Veľký a Malý Zajf ½ h -

Občasný prameň ½ h - Havrania skala ½ h - Občasný prameň ¼ h - Stratená ¾ h - Stratenská píla ¼ - Dedinky ¾ h.
Total: 4 ¾ hours. **Elevation gain:** 368 m.
Map: Slovenský raj 1 : 50 000 (sheet 124), VKÚ, š. p., Harmanec.

Classification: Easy and slightly demanding circle. Only the short ascent to the Geravy plateau and the stretch from Občasný prameň spring to Havrania skala rock is a bit demanding. The remaining stretches are in easy and well-marked terrain. Nevertheless, pay attention to the changing colour of marking.
Basic route: The tour will introduce you to diverse sights of the southern part of the Slovenský raj Mts. You will ascend to the karstic plateau of Geravy, walk in attractive environment of the Nature Reserve of Malé Zajfy and around the natural phenomenon of the Občasný prameň spring. You will also ascend to the top of the Havrania skala rock with its nice views of the surrounding landscape. In the final part of the trip you will visit the mountain mining village of Stratená with its romantic setting.

Start at the village of **Dedinky** (795 m) following the green mark (5723), which heads up the village around the church. It continues through the meadows passing below the Gačovské skaly rocks and later in forest below the chair ski lift. You will ascend as far as the station of the ski lift, unless you make it easier for yourself and have a ride instead of walking. The upper station of the lift has the snack bar open both in summer and winter seasons. Continue from the crossroads of **Geravy** (1,032 m) on the yellow-marked path (8769) heading to the west. This mark is parallel to the red mark (0910) but after a short walk you will have to turn left to steeper terrain, which leads to the **Malý Zajf** crossroads (900 m). Continue slightly ascending on the yellow-marked path in a nice grassy valley of Malý Zajf. At the crossroads called **Veľký a Malý Zajf** (818 m) turn right sticking to the yellow mark. Now you are ascending in the Veľký Zajf valley on narrow asphalt road. Shortly after turn left and walk above the brook and there is a steeper ascent to the natural phenomenon of the **Občasný prameň** spring (960 m) Continue ascending on the yellow-marked path up to the top of the **Havrania skala** rock (1,153 m) with steep rock faces. Wonderful view of the plateaux of the Slovenský raj Mts. and the surrounding mountain ranges is the reward. The route returns then down to the Občasný prameň spring and continues on the green mark (5727) traversing the forest below the Havrania skala rock as far as a meadow. The route continues in the forest and then it descends to the village of **Stratená** (805 m). Leaving the village behind continue through the Stratenská dolina valley eastward following the red mark (0908) on the left bank of the Hnilec. There is asphalt road as far as the Stratenská píla. The charming environs of the cottage settlement are enhanced by the narrow bottom of the valley filled with water of the Palcmanská Maša reservoir. Passing the **Stratenská píla** crossroads (785 m) continue on the red-marked path. You are now walking on the bank of the water reservoir and a short ascent through the forest will lead you back to the village of **Dedinky**.

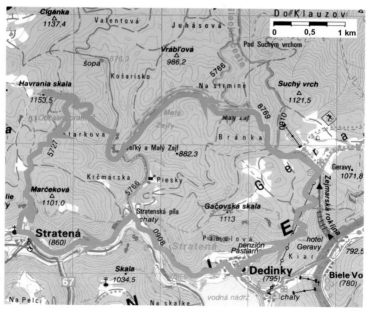

14 The valley of Tiesňavy

Dedinky – Stratená – Tiesňavy – Dobšinská ľadová jaskyňa – Stratenský kaňon – Stratená – Dedinky

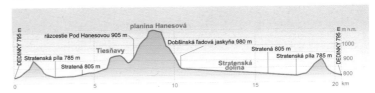

Situation: The Slovenský raj Mts. - South (western part)

Starting and finishing point: Dedinky, bus stop, railway station, parking lot.

Time schedule: Dedinky - Stratenská píla ¾ h - Stratená ¼ h - Pod Hanesovou 1 h - Dobšinská ľadová jaskyňa 1 h - Kri-vian ½ h - Stratenský kaňon ½ h - Stratená ½ h - Dedinky 1 h.

Total: 5 ½ hours.

Elevation gain: 120 m.

Map: Slovenský raj 1 : 50 000 (sheet 124), VKÚ, š. p., Harmanec.

Classification: Medium difficult and demanding tour in a form of circle. The stretch in the valley of Tiesňavy is somewhat more demanding and it is secured by climbing aids.

Basic route: The tour runs in the southern part of the National Park of Slovenský raj, which is rich in karstic phenomena. Its initial part leads through the picturesque environment of the Stratenská píla along the taper-

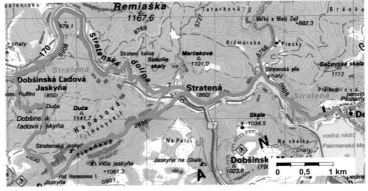

Dobšinská ľadová jaskyňa cave

ing water reservoir of Palcmanská Maša. Later it continues through the canyon-like Tiesňavy valley and the Nature Reserve of Stratená. It returns to the Stratenská dolina valley and passes by its gem, the Stratenský kaňon canyon, descends by the national natural phenomenon of the Dobšinská ľadová jaskyňa cave and ends in the village of Dedinky.

Start in **Dedinky** (795 m) taking the red-marked path (0908) heading to the west. Walking on forest path, which runs above the Palcmanská Maša water reservoir you will draw close to it when you reach the **Stratenská píla** (785 m). Continue on the red-marked narrow asphalt road to the village of **Stratená** (805 m). Passing the crossroads turn left following the blue mark (2830). You will ascend in nice canyon-shaped valley of **Tiesňavy** secured by wooden footbridges and climbing aids advancing along the brook. The final part of the ascent is more demanding and having it climbed you reach the crossroads of **Pod Hanesovou** (905 m), which is in an open grassy plateau called Hanesová. Continue on blue mark mostly in forest towards the **Dobšinská ľadová jaskyňa.** You should interrupt the tour here and see this unique cave. After the break carry on in the direction of the eponymous village: Dobšinská Ľadová Jaskyňa. Then continue down the Stratenská dolina valley following the red mark (0908) along the state road. Before reaching the road tunnel turn left to narrow asphalt road passing through the picturesque Stratenský kaňon canyon. Then you will be again walking along the state road to the village of **Stratená** (805 m). The return trip to **Dedinky** is the same as described at the beginning of the trip.

15 The Geravy plateau and Tomášovská Belá

Dedinky – Geravy – Predný Hýľ – Klauzy – Tomášovská Belá – Čingov

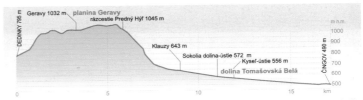

Situation: The Slovenský raj Mts. - East.
Starting point: Dedinky, bus stop, railway station, parking lot.
Finishing point: Čingov, bus stop, parking lot.
Time schedule: Dedinky - Geravy ¾ h -

Predný Hýľ ¾ h - Klauzy 1 h - Sokolia dolina ¾ h - Kyseľ ½ h - Biely potok ¾ h - Čingov ½ h. **Total:** 5 hours.
Elevation gain: 555 m.
Map: Slovenský raj 1 : 50 000 (sheet 124), VKÚ, š. p., Harmanec.

Classification: Moderately difficult trip. Steep ascent to the Geravy plateau and some stretches of the Tomášovská Belá valley secured by wooden climbing aids are demanding.
Basic route: The tour runs in the picturesque environment of the Slovenský raj Mts. First it leads across the extensive karstic plateau of Geravy. The final stretch of the trip is in the widened part of the gorge of Prielom Hornádu.

The whole route is marked in green (5733). Start at the village of **Dedinky** (795 m) and walk up around the church. Continue through the meadows below the Gačovská skala rock. Enter the forest and ascend on the path leading below the ski lift. The ascent becomes more comfortable at the edge of the **Geravy** plateau, the meadows of which, especially in spring months, are in full bloom. Leaving behind the crossroads (1,032 m) next to the top station of the ski lift continue on comfortable forest road passing through more meadows of the plateau. At the edge of the plateau at the crossroads of **Predný Hýľ** (1,045 m) abandon the forest road and continue to the left up the forest path. Steep descent below the Holý Kameň to the little valley of Berezinec follows. Continue along the brook to enter a more distinct forest road, which is also more comfortable. It leads to the water reservoir of **Klauzy** (643 m). The following stretch of the tour is in the attractive environs of the reservoir and you are ascending accompanied by clear water of the Biely potok brook. By this time you have reached the narrow forested valley of Tomášovská Belá. Walk alternatively on both sides of the brook as far as the crossroads of **Sokolia dolina-ústie** (572 m). Continue walking right in the channel of the brook secured by climbing aids. You will get to the crossroads **Kyseľ-ústie** (55 6 m).

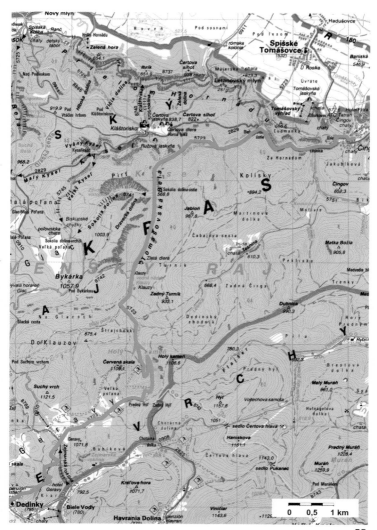

Novy mlyn

Spišská Koliba

Ranč

Hrad Hornádu

Rоveň 521,5

Pod sosnami

Pod lesom

Hadušovce

SOK

chaty detský tábor

Zelená hora 654,1

Spišské Tomášovce (532)

180

Nad Podleskom

thrik 651,8

Čertova sihoť

Majerská chata

römska kolónia

Baniská 546,9

B737

Letanovský mlyn

U Rosika

919,9 Pod Vtáčím hrbom

Pod Kláštoriskom

Vltča dolina

Čertova dolina

Zelená dolina

Čertova sihoť 822

Uvrate

Tomášovské jaskyňa

Tomášovský výhľad

chata

hotel Flóra

Robinkovská TO

Čingov

chaty

S

Čertova jaskyňa 838,7

Čertova diera

Horná lúčka

Kláštoriská

Ľudmanka

Ružová jaskyňa

Vyšný Kyseľ

Za Hornádom

lesnica

Čingov

Jakublová

Čingov 652,3

968,2

Malý Kysel

Prielom Hornáda

Kolísky

S

575r

894,2

Biskupské chýžky

Sokolia dolina

Sokolia dolina-ústie 568,8

Jabloň 987,8

Martinova dolka

Matka Božia 905,8

poľovnícka chata

Sokolia dolina-vrchol

Veľká poľana

1003,9

Zlatá diera

Čabalová cesta

buda lesina

chata

810,3

Peklisko

Medvedia

Bykárka 1057,9

Pod Bykárkou

Klauzy

Turnik

Zadný Turnik 933,1

668,4

Zadná Čirga

Dubnica 990,3

Trenky

Na Glacoch

Glacká cesta

675,4

Štrajcháki

Dedinský chodník

780,3

Horné Predmu

Do Klauzov

Holý kameň 1106,6

Flašer

892,3

Breslová dolka

Pod Suchým vrchom

Červená skala 1108,1

Malý Muráň 961,0

Suchý vrch 1121,5

Veľká poľana

Predný Hýľ Zadný Hýľ

Hýľ 1157,8

Vojtechova samota

Hnilčanova dolka

Chotárna dolina

1051

sedlo Čertova hlava

Geravy 1071,8

Chotárna dolka

Babíková

Zejmarská roklina

Haniskova 1101,1

Čertova hlava 1143,0

sedlo Pukanec

Predný Muráň 1228,4

Dedinky (798)

hotel penzión

Kráľova hora 1071,7

Biele Vody (780)

Havrania Dolina

Viničiar 1143,5

penzión Havran

Muráň 1259,9

Pod Muráňom

0   0,5   1 km

Geravy

The climbing aids including chains and little footbridges will help you to get to the point where the Biely potok brook flows into the Hornád river. Leaving the crossroads behind (510 m) continue walking below the rock gallery of the Tomášovský výhľad to the widened part of the Prielom Hornádu gorge. The final stretch of the comfortable forest road below the rocks called Ihla and Kazateľnica passes by the place where the Lesnica brook mouths into the widened part of the Prielom Hornádu gorge and you will find yourself at the recreation centre of **Čingov** (490 m).

16 The plateaux of the Slovenský raj Mts.

Dedinky – Geravy – Glac – Malá poľana – Palc – Píla – Podlesok

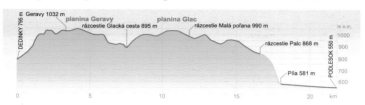

Situation: The Slovenský raj Mts. - West.
Starting point: Dedinky, bus stop, railway station, parking lot.
Finishing point: Podlesok, bus stop, parking lot.
Time schedule: Dedinky - Geravy ¾ h - Pod Suchým vrchom ¾ h - Glacká cesta ¼ h - Glac ¼ h - Malá poľana ½ h - Palc 1 h - Píla ¼ h - Podlesok 1 h.
Total: 4 ¾ hours.
Elevation gain: 482 m.
Map: Slovenský raj 1 : 50 000 (sheet 124), VKÚ, š. p., Harmanec.

Classification: Moderately difficult route. Steep ascent to the Geravy plateau is the difficult part. The rest of the trip is in comfortable terrain.
Basic route: This route connects the recreation centres of Dedinky and Podlesok, it crosses the attractive environment of meadows and forests of the two most expressive plateaux of the Slovenský raj Mts.

The trip starts at the village of **Dedinky** (795 m) following the green hiking mark (5723), which heads to the north-east. Walk up the village by the church and later through the meadow below the Gačovská skala rock. The path going through the forest below the chair lift becomes steeper. Its final part at the edge of the **Geravy** plateau (1,032 m) becomes easier. Once you reach the crossroads at the top station of the chair lift continue following the red mark (0910) north-westward. The first part of the road leads through meadows along with the yellow hiking mark. After you reach the edge of the plateau turn right and continue through the forest on the red mark (0910). The forest road traverses the western slope of the plateau. Later the trail runs up the path to the crossroads of **Pod Suchým vrchom** (930 m). Turn right and continue on the comfortable Glacká cesta road and later on path sticking to the red mark. Short ascent to the **Glac** plateau (990 m) comes after the crossroads of the **Glacká cesta** road (895 m). Walking through the meadow by the well and a former gamekeeper's lodge you will pass to the forested undulated terrain of the plateau. A meadow with the crossroads of **Malá poľana** (990 m) follows. This is the place where you abandon the Glacká cesta road, formerly used as the trade road between the regions of Gemer and Spiš

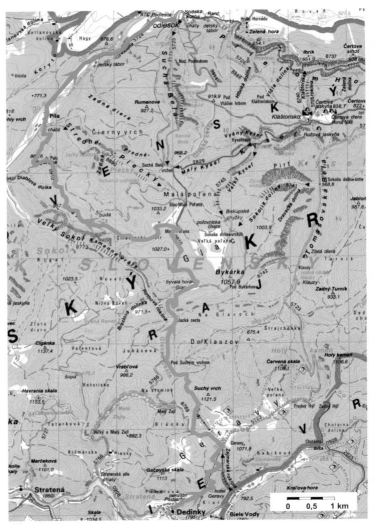

Palc

and turn left descending down the red-marked (0910) trail running along the edge of the meadow. The continuous descent runs on the Palc crest, which offers fine views of the environs of the Veľký Sokol gorge. You will soon descend down the forested slope to the **Palc** crossroads (868 m). Turn right onto the yellow-marked path there and continue on forest road as far as the settlement of **Píla** (581 m) in the valley of the Veľká Biela voda brook. Forested slopes skirt the attractive V-shaped valley. It has a wide bottom with a brook. Continue on comfortable green-marked (5724) trail. Cross the village and enter asphalt road, which turns right and descends down the edge of the valley. Turn right again onto the path running along the brook. In the tapered end of the valley you have to pass through a short gorge called Tesnina secured by artificial climbing aids. At its end you will come out of the forest to the open landscape at the edge of the Hornádska kotlina basin. Continue along the brook to the recreation centre of **Podlesok** (550 m).

17 From Dedinky to Novoveská Huta

Dedinky – Biele Vody – Čertova hlava – Rybník – Novoveská Huta

Situation: The Slovenský raj Mts. - East.
Starting point: Dedinky, bus stop, railway station, parking lot.
Finishing point: Novoveská Huta, bus stop, parking lot.
Time schedule: Dedinky - Biele Vody

½ h - Chotárna dolka ½ h - sedlo Čertova hlava ½ h - Novoveská Huta 1 ½ h.
Total: 3 hours.
Elevation gain: 491 m.
Map: Slovenský raj 1 : 50 000 (sheet 124), VKÚ, š. p., Harmanec.

Classification: Easy route with only one demanding ascent to the saddle of Čertova hlava and a rather steep beginning of the descent from the saddle. The rest of the route runs in undemanding terrain, mostly on well-marked forest roads.
Basic route: The route starts in the attractive environment of the forest surrounding the water reservoir of Palcmanská Maša. It ascends to the grassy

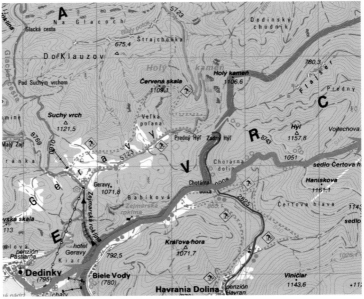

saddle of Okrúhla jama, crossroads of Chotárna dolka and the Čertova hlava saddle. The second part of the route is a comfortable descent around the small water reservoir at Vojtechova samota and across the wide grassy valley of the Holubnica brook.

The route starts in the village of **Dedinky** (795 m) and follows the red hiking mark (0908) first heading to the south-east along the Palcmanská Maša water reservoir. The first stretch of the trip is on asphalt road. Turn left up along the recreation centres. Continue shortly in the forest and following the edge of the ski track descend to the valley of **Biele Vody** (780 m). The field road runs below the national Nature Reserve of Zejmarská roklina with the Bielovodské skaly limestone rocks. The road leads up to the meadow saddle of Okrúhla jama. Its name (The Round Hole) suggests the existence of karstic phenomena in this area, namely sinkholes. Leaving the saddle behind walk down towards the **Chotárna dolka** crossroads (880 m). This is where the steep ascent up the forest path to the **Čertova hlava** saddle (1,051 m) starts. The saddle provides wonderful views of the southern part of the Slovenský raj Mts. and the Hornádska kotlina basin. After a short rest in the saddle, which is the highest point of your route, continue by milder and later steeper descent down

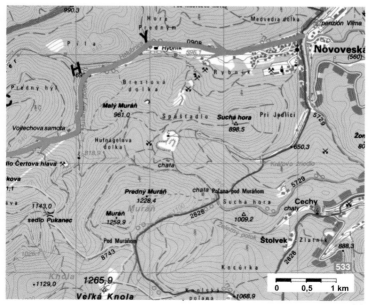

the red mark. Pass by a well into more open terrain near the water reservoir in the locality called Vojtechova samota. A comfortable stretch through the forest following the track of the former forest railway as far as the narrow asphalt road comes next. After a short walk on asphalt road turn right and passing by the locality of Rybník you will enter a nice grassy valley. It is very near to the end of your trip in **Novoveská Huta** (560 m).

Palcmanská Maša

18 From Dedinky to Dobšiná

Dedinky – Palcmanská Maša – Dobšinský kopec – Voniarky – Dobšiná

Situation: The Volovské vrchy Mts. - West
Starting point: Dedinky, bus stop, railway station, parking lot.
Finishing point: Dobšiná, bus stop, parking lot.
Time schedule: Dedinky - Palcmanská

Maša ½ h - Dobšinský kopec ½ h - Voniarky ¾ h - Dobšiná 1 ¼ h.
Total: 3 hours.
Elevation gain: 447 m.
Map: Slovenský raj 1 : 50 000 (sheet 124), VKÚ, š. p., Harmanec.

Classification: Easy tour. What may be demanding is the steep descent from Voniarky to Dobšiná. The well-marked trail runs mostly in the forests. Pay attention to the stretches passing along the state road and to the changing colour of marking.
Basic route: This comfortable route cutting the westernmost crest of the Volovské vrchy Mts.

Voniarky

Start at the village of **Dedinky** (795 m). The route follows the green mark (5723) heading south-eastward. Walk on the state road along the water reservoir of the Palcmanská Maša. You will come to the wall of the dam and later to the crossroads next to the railway station of Dedinky. Turn left there

and descend along the blue mark (2825) to the crossroads of **Palcmanská Maša**. Turn right here to underpass and shortly after turn left to follow the yellow mark (8745). Now you ascend the meadow towards the **Dobšinský kopec** crossroads (851 m). Continue ascending to the saddle below the Dobšinský kopec Mt. Follow the red mark (0901) to the right along the state road. At the foothill turn left onto the forest road. Now you walk on the distinct ridge running along the southern border of the National Park of the Slovenský raj Mts. with beautiful views of both the southern and northern sides. After the moderate ascent in the forest up the ridge and later in undulated half-open terrain you will reach the **Voniarky** crossroads (915 m), which is also the highest point of this route. Now you are at the edge of the attractive grassy plateau of Voniarky adorned by islands of coniferous trees. Abandon the ridge and descend to Dobšiná. Continue downward following the blue mark (2830). The descent, apart from the views, is also interesting for the changing composition of the forest. Descend first on forest path and then on forest road gradually entering a more open terrain. In the final part of the descent you will leave the road, turn right and continue straight ahead through the meadows until you reach **Dobšiná** (468 m). The trip ends next to the bus station.

Above Dobšiná

19 To the ridge of the western part of the Volovské vrchy Mts.

Dedinky – Dobšinský kopec – Kruhová – Dobšinský vrch – Súľová – Hnilec

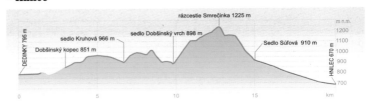

Situation: The Volovské vrchy Mts. - West
Starting point: Dedinky, bus stop, railway station, parking lot.
Finishing point: Hnilec, bus stop, parking lot.
Time schedule: Dedinky - Palcmanská Maša ½ h - Dobšinský kopec ½ h -

Kruhová ½ h - Dobšinský vrch 1 h - Smrečinka 2 ¼ h - Súľová ½ h - Hnilec ¾ h.
Total: 6 hours.
Elevation gain: 503 m.
Map: Slovenský raj 1 : 50 000 (sheet 124), VKÚ, š. p., Harmanec.

Classification: Moderately difficult and comparatively long route. It runs mostly on quality forest roads with good marking. The first and last parts of the trip run along the state road and require caution.

Basic route: The route starts at the picturesque mountain environment next to the water reservoir of Palcmanská Maša. It ascends to and passes on the ridge, which separates the region of Spiš from that of Gemer. The border of the protective belt of the National park of the Slovenský raj Mts. also passes through the ridge. Its relief facilitates the passage and offers nice views of the environs of the Hnilecká dolina valley and a great part of the northern Gemer.

The route starts in the village of **Dedinky** (795 m) and follows the green hiking mark (5723) south-eastward. Stick to the state road leading next to the water reservoir of Palcmanská Maša. You will come to the wall of the dam and later to the crossroads next to the railway station of Dedinky. Turn left there and descend along the blue mark (2825) to the crossroads of Palcmanská Maša. Turn right here to underpass and shortly after turn left to follow the yellow mark (8745). Now you ascend the meadow towards the Dobšinský kopec crossroads (851 m). You are ascending to the crest below the **Dobšinský kopec Mt**. Fine views of the environs will accompany you also along the next part of the trip. Turn left at the Dobšinský kopec crossroads and continue eastward on the red-marked (0901) trail. As you ascend to the crest you pass through undulated terrain above the ski track drawing closer to the **Kruhová** saddle (966 m). Continue on the red-marked path and slightly descend through meadows and forest to the easily discernible saddle of the **Dobšinský vrch Mt.** (898 m). Ascend in the undulated terrain and keep following the red mark. The path runs mostly in forests, meadows and clearings offering several nice views. The ascent ends at the **Smrečinka** crossroads (1,225 m), the highest point of the route. The descent in forest ends in a meadow. After a short ascent continue as far as the crossroads called **Súľová** saddle (910 m). At this point abandon the marked hiking trail and turn left onto the state road. Descend down the road and after a while you will reach the final point of the trip, the village of **Hnilec** (722 m) where you can have some refreshment.

The view of the Hnilec from Súľová

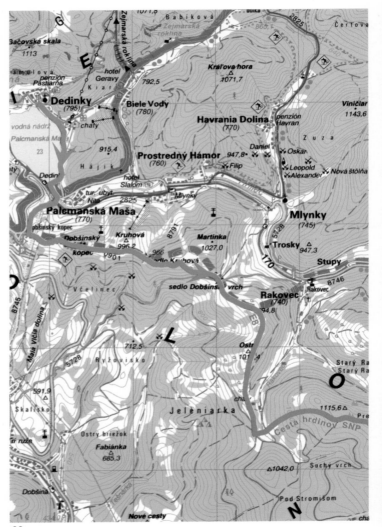

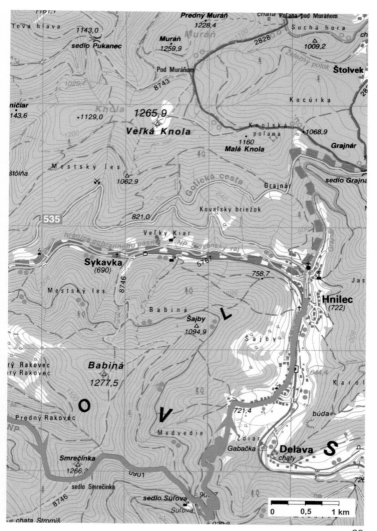

20 The Dobšinská ľadová jaskyňa cave

Dedinky – Palcmanská Maša – Dobšinský kopec – Voniarky – Pod Hanesovou II. – Nižná záhrada – Dobšinská ľadová jaskyňa

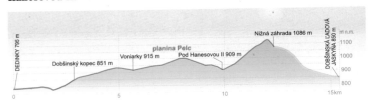

Situation: The Slovenský raj Mts. - South, the Volovské vrchy Mts. - West

Starting point: Dedinky, bus stop, railway station, parking lot.

Finishing point: Dobšinská ľadová jaskyňa, bus stop, parking lot.

Time schedule: Dedinky - Palcmanská Maša ½ h - Dobšinský kopec ½ h - Voniarky ¾ h - Pod Hanesovou II. 1 ¾ h - Nižná záhrada 1 h - Dobšinská ľadová jaskyňa ¾ h.

Total: 5 ¼ hours.

Elevation gain: 291 m.

Map: Slovenský raj 1 : 50 000 (sheet 124), VKÚ, š. p., Harmanec.

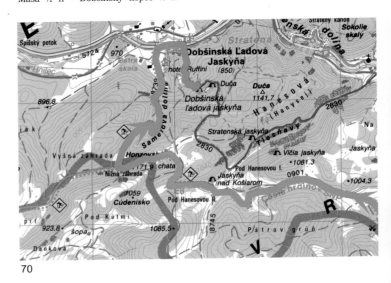

Classification: Moderately difficult and demanding tour. Although there are no difficult ascents it is comparatively long. It runs in comfortable terrain mostly on well-marked forest roads.

Basic route: The route starts in the picturesque environs of the Palcmanská Maša water reservoir and ascends the ridge at the boundary of the regions of Spiš and Gemer. Comfortable passage on the undulated wide ridge offers plenty of views of the Stratenská dolina valley and its environs including the northern Gemer. The descent heads to the Stratenská dolina valley.

The trip starts at the village of **Dedinky** (795 m) and follows the green mark (5723) south-eastward. Walk on the state road along the water reservoir of the Palcmanská Maša. You will come to the wall of the dam and later to the crossroads next to the railway station of Dedinky. Turn left there and descend along the blue mark (2825) to the crossroads of Palcmanská Maša. Turn right here to underpass and shortly after turn left to follow the yellow mark (8745). Now you ascend the meadow towards the **Dobšinský kopec** crossroads (851 m). Continue on the red mark (0901) to the right and up along the state road. When you reach the foothill turn left on to the forest road. Walk on a crest along the southern border of the National Park of the Slovenský raj Mts. with fine views of both southern and northern sides. After moderate ascent in the forest up the ridge and later in undulated half-open terrain you will reach the **Voniarky** crossroads (915 m), which is also the highest point of this route. Now you are at the edge of the attractive grassy

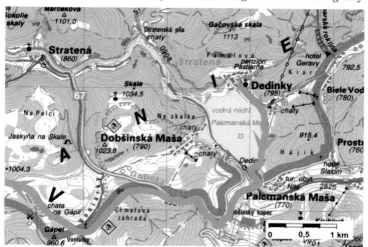

Dobšinská ľadová jaskyňa cave

plateau of Voniarky. Continue along its foot to a grassy kettle sticking to the red mark. Traverse towards the narrow asphalt road and turn left below the karstic plateau of Pelc. Soon after take the forest road heading through the saddle between the Čierna hora Mt. and the Pelc plateau to the meadows of Hanesová plateau as far as the **Pod Hanesovou II.** crossroads (909 m). The route continues on the red mark. Moderate ascent in undulated terrain follows. Avoiding the top of the Honzovské Mt. (1,172 m) you will arrive at the alpine meadow at the **Nižná záhrada** saddle (1,086 m), the highest point of the route. Now abandon the crest and turn right following the yellow mark (8739). Descend to the Samelova dolina valley. The continuous moderate descent on forest road ends next to the state road. Turn right there and after a short walk on the road you will find yourself in the village of Dobšinská Ľadová Jaskyňa (850 m). Above the village is the eponymous cave, which is the aim of the trip. The blue marked trail (2830) leads to it. The cave is the national nature phenomenon and its visit certainly means refreshment especially in hot summer months.

21 The Havrania skala rock from Stratená

Stratená – Občasný prameň – Havrania skala – Stratenský kaňon – Dobšinská Ľadová Jaskyňa

Situation: The Slovenský raj Mts. - South (western part)
Starting point: Stratená, bus stop, railway station, parking lot.
Finishing point: Dobšinská Ľadová Jaskyňa, bus stop, parking lot.
Time schedule: Stratená - Občasný prameň 1 h - Havrania skala ½ h - Stratenský kaňon ¾ h - Krivian ½ h - Dobšinská Ľadová Jaskyňa ½ h.
Total: 3 ¼ hours.
Elevation gain: 339 m.
Map: Slovenský raj 1 : 50 000 (sheet 124), VKÚ, š. p., Harmanec.

Classification: Easy tour. Only some steeper stretches of the ascent to the Havrania skala from Stratená are a bit toilsome. The trail is on paths and forest roads. The final stretch between the Stratenský kaňon canyon running along the busy state road requires caution.
Basic route: The trip introduces the hiker to the most attractive parts of the south of the National Park of Slovenský raj Mts. Conservationists constantly monitor its precious localities. The trail runs in great part of the National Nature Reserve of Stratená. It ascends to the natural phenomenon of the Občasný prameň spring. The exciting part of the trip is the ascent to the top of Havrania skala rock.

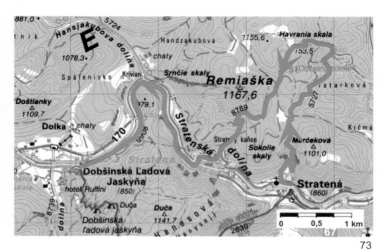

The route starts at the village of **Stratená** (805 m) and heading to the north it follows the green mark (5727). Walk up the village towards the cemetery, then through a meadow to the forest. The path ascends in an incision between the Sokolie skaly rocks and Marčeková to a less demanding terrain as far as a meadow. Continue on forest road traversing below the Havrania skala rock before you arrive at the **Občasný prameň** crossroads (960 m). As the name of the spring suggests (Občasný means intermittent in English) it appears on the surface in irregular intervals. Leaving the spring behind continue to the left on a steep path following the yellow mark (8769) as far as the **Havrania skala** rock (1,154 m), the highest point of the route. This dominant rock at the edge of the Lipovecká karstic plateau is part of Nature Reserve bearing the same name. It provides far-reaching views of the southern part of the regions of Spiš and the northern Gemer. Having enjoyed them, continue down on the yellow mark (8769). Descend

Stratenský kaňon canyon

down the Lipovecká planina plateau and later on forest road. When you reach the end of the road turn left onto a steeper descending path and continue on it until you reach the narrow asphalt road leading to the **Stratenský kaňon** canyon (815 m). Continue comfortably to the right on the red mark (0908). You will arrive to road tunnel and turn right along the state road passing by the **Krivian** crossroads (840 m) as far as the aim of the trip: the village of **Dobšinská Ľadová Jaskyňa**. Those who are interested can continue farther following the blue mark (2830), which leads to the world famous Dobšinská ľadová jaskyňa cave. The ascent to the cave takes about twenty minutes. After seeing the cave you will perhaps appreciate refreshment available next to the cave or in the village.

22 The western part of the Slovenský raj Mts.

Stratená – Stratenský kaňon – Krivian – Kopanec – Blajzloch – Vernár

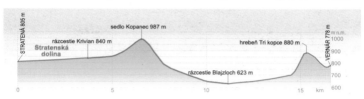

Situation: The Slovenský raj Mts. - South (western part)
Starting point: Stratená, bus stop, railway station, parking lot.
Finishing point: Vernár, bus stop, parking lot.
Time schedule: Stratená - Stratenský

kaňon ½ h - Krivian ½ h - Kopanec ¾ h - Blajzloch 1 h - Vernár 1 ½ h.
Total: 4 ¼ hours.
Elevation gain: 364 m.
Map: Slovenský raj 1 : 50 000 (sheet 124), VKÚ, š. p., Harmanec.

Classification: Moderately difficult tour. It contains steep ascent to the crest of Tri kopce Mt. in the conclusion of the trip. The rest of the route is in comfortable terrain alternatively on asphalt roads, forest roads and forest paths. Orientation is easy thanks to good marking.

Basic route: The route runs in the attractive Stratenská dolina valley. Its most beautiful stretch is the short gorge of the Stratenský kaňon canyon. The route continues in the forested Hanzjakubova dolina valley, it heads to the valley of the Veľká Biela voda brook and passes through the narrow forested stretch of the valley. Finally it leads to the crest of the Tri kopce Mts. and passing through he valley of the Vernársky potok brook it ends below the slopes of the Nízke Tatry Mts. in Vernár.

The trip starts at the village of **Stratená** (805 m) and follows the red mark (0908) to the west. It runs along the state road to road tunnel. Turn right there and cross the **Stratenský kaňon** canyon (815 m). Continue along the road as far the crossroads of **Krivian** (840 m). Abandon the red mark and follow the green trail (5724) turning to the right and upwards. This part of the route leads to the lateral forested Hanzjakubova dolina valley, which has a small water reservoir. Continue first on asphalt road, later turn right and walk on forest road as far as the grassy sedlo **Kopanec** saddle (987 m). The foot of the valley is adorned by wide meadows lying around the above-mentioned saddle. Continue down the forest path, which leads later along the brook. Now you walk around the romantic nook of the small water reservoir called Blajzloch with cottages. Finally you arrive to the Veľká Biela voda valley and the **Blajz-**

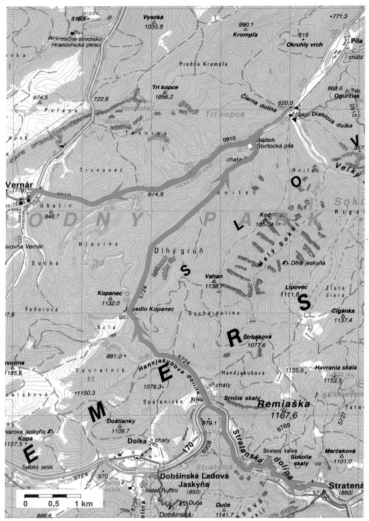

Vernárska tiesňava gorge

loch crossroads (623 m). Turn left here and continue on red mark (0910) on narrow asphalt road. After about 30 minutes the turning to the red-marked forest roads follows and the trail joins the brook. Later ascend to the right up the slope to the forested crest of the Tri kopce Mt. Finally descend down the forest and meadow to the valley of the Vernársky potok brook. The trip ends in the typical Slovak village of **Vernár** (778 m) giving opportunity of relaxing and refreshment.

23 Around Mlynky

Mlynky – Chotárna dolka – Dedinky – Palcmanská Maša – Mlynky

Situation: The Slovenský raj Mts. - South, the Volovské vrchy Mts. - West
Starting and finishing point: Prostredný Hámor, bus stop, railway station, parking lot.
Time schedule: Prostredný Hámor - Havrania Dolina ½ h - Chotárna dolka

¾ h - Biele Vody ½ h - Dedinky ½ h - Palcmanská Maša ¼ h - Prostredný Hámor ½ h.
Total: 3 hours.
Elevation gain: 141 m.
Map: Slovenský raj 1 : 50 000 (sheet 124), VKÚ, š. p., Harmanec.

Classification: Easy circle on asphalt and forest roads. Thanks to quality marking orientation is easy.
Basic route: The route consists of a comfortable passage through the southern part of the National Park Slovenský raj and its protective belt. It runs up the nice Havrania dolina valley with forested slopes and grassy bottom. In its second part it passes through the National Nature Reserve of Zejmarská roklina adorned by the Bielovodské skaly limestone rocks. Comfortable path will carry you to the Palcmanská Maša water reservoir.

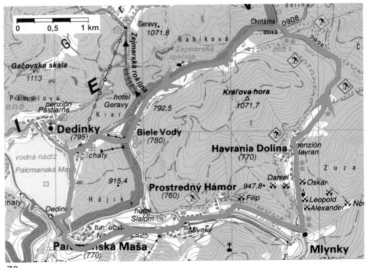

Start at the village of **Prostredný Hámor** (760 m), which is the subsidiary part of the village of Mlynky. The trip follows the blue-marked trail (2825) heading to the east. First you walk comfortably along the state road. At the Mlynky-Havrania dolina crossroads (739 m) turn left and moderately ascend up the Havrania dolina valley on narrow asphalt road. You will arrive at the village of **Havrania Dolina** (770), also part of the village of Mlynky. It has a remarkable folk architecture. The road runs first in the wider part of the valley and later through its tapering slightly up to the **Chotárna dolka** crossroads (880 m), the highest point of the route. Turn left onto the red-marked forest road (0908). Continue ascending to the grassy saddle of Okrúhla jama. You can see karstic sinkholes there. Carry on down the meadows below the Bielovodské skaly rocks, which are situated in

Mlynky

the Nature Reserve of Zejmarská roklina. Soon after you will find yourself in locality **Biele Vody** (780 m), which is another of the settlements forming part of the village of Mlynky. Continue on the edge of the ski track shortly upwards and then descend in the forest to the recreation centre of **Dedinky** (795 m). The route continues from the crossroads in front of the hotel to the left following the green mark (5723). Now you are walking comfortably along the state road on the bank of the Palcmanská Maša water reservoir. You are drawing closer to the railway station of Dedinky via the wall of the dam. Turn left and following the blue mark you will arrive at the crossroads on the edge of the **Palcmanská Maša** village (770). Turn right to underpass and immediately after turn left onto the field road. This road leads above the railway track. Finally cross the track. The road leads to the roadhouse at **Prostredný Hámor** where you can conclude the trip having a glass of juice or beer.

24 From Mlynky to Dobšiná

Mlynky – Kruhová – Dobšinský kopec – Dobšiná – Dobšinský vrch – Mlynky

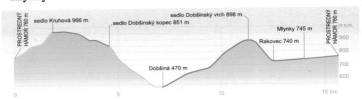

Situation: The Volovské vrchy Mts. - West
Starting and finishing point: Prostredný Hámor, bus stop, railway station, parking lot.
Time schedule: Prostredný Hámor - Kruhová ½ h - Dobšiná 1 ½ h - Dobšinský vrch 1 ½ h - Rakovec ½ h - Havrania Dolina ¼ h - Prostredný Hámor ½ h.
Total: 4 ¾ hours.
Elevation gain: 498 m.
Map: Slovenský raj 1 : 50 000 (sheet 124), VKÚ, š. p., Harmanec.

Classification: Moderately difficult route with long and demanding ascent from Dobšiná to the ridge of the Volovské vrchy Mts. It mostly leads on forest roads and paths.
Basic route: This circle passes from the Hnilecká dolina valley across the ridge of the Volovské vrchy Mts. to the valley of the Dobšinský potok brook. Then it returns back to the protective belt of the National Park of the Slovenský raj Mts.

Start at the village of **Prostredný Hámor** (760 m) next to the municipal office. The route heads to the south and follows the yellow mark (8791). Walk on the road leading above the railway track and up the village. Then ascend the meadows and ski tracks and at the conclusion of this stretch there is a steeper ascent to alpine meadow and the **Kruhová** saddle (966 m), the highest point of the trip. Turn right there and continue on the red mark (0901). Walking on undulated crest pass above the ski tracks. Later you will pass below the Dobšinský kopec Mt. and go down to the crossroads called **Dobšinský kopec** saddle (851m) Continue from this place turning left now descending on the yellow-marked trail (8745). You will certainly appreciate wonderful views of the river Slaná valley lying below. The route heads now almost directly downward and crosses the state road several times. The trail descends parallel to the underground piping, which supplies water of the Palcmanská Maša reservoir to the water power station in Dobšiná. Soon you will find yourself at the edge of the town **Dobšiná** (468 m). Once you get bellow the power station turn left onto asphalt road and walk down the suburb. After a while take the sharp left turning to join the green marked-trail (5728), which heads to the Dobšinský vrch Mt. The crossroads of Dobšiná with indication of trails and places is about 10 minute walk away from this crossroads of yellow and green marks. Your trail continues by long ascent up to the head of the Tešnárka valley. Continue on forest roads and shortly on narrow asphalt road. While you are ascending on old mining roads you can observe the traces left here by the past mining activities. At the end of the ascent is the well discernible saddle of **Dobšinský vrch** (898 m). Continue on the green mark and descend comfortably down the forest road as far as the Hnilecká dolina valley. Turn left at the Mlynky-Rakovec crossroads and follow the green mark on asphalt road as far as the **Mlynky-Havrania Dolina** crossroads. Turn left there and continue following the blue mark (2825). Walk first on the edge of the valley and later the path changes into the state road, which leads to the aim of the trip, part of Mlynky called **Prostredný Hámor.**

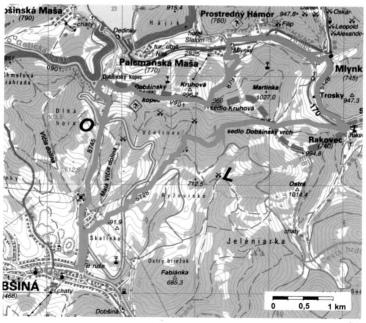

25 The Babiná Mt.

Mlynky – Dobšinský vrch – Smrečinka – Babiná – Mlynky

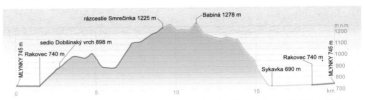

Situation: The Volovské vrchy Mts. - West.
Starting and finishing point: Mlynky, bus stop, railway station, parking lot.
Time schedule: Mlynky - Rakovec ¼ h - Dobšinský vrch ¾ h - Smrečinka 2 ¼ h - Babiná ¾ h - Sykavka 1 ¼ h - Rakovec ¾ h - Mlynky ¼ h. **Total:** 6 ¼ hours.
Elevation gain: 588 m.
Map: Slovenský raj 1 : 50 000 (sheet 124), VKÚ, š. p., Harmanec.

Classification: Moderately difficult circle. Especially the continuous ascent from Rakovec to Babiná can be toilsome. The route runs on forest roads and paths. Its marking is a bit deficient in the part called Smrečinka-Babiná-Sykavka, so please, pay attention.
Basic route: The route ascends to the ridge separating the regions of Spiš and Gemer. It continues through the forest and meadows on top of the ridge with views of wide environs.

The trip starts in the village of **Mlynky** (745 m) near the church at the crossroads Mlynky-Havrania Dolina (739 m). It follows the green hiking mark (5728). Walk along the state road. After a while turn right onto narrow asphalt road leading to the village of Rakovec and walk on it as far as the **Mlynky-Rakovec** crossroads. Continue to underpass following the green mark. Beyond the underpass continue to the right and ascend the narrow forest road leaving the village of Rakovec behind. At this point continuous ascent in half-open terrain starts and ends at the saddle of the **Dobšinský vrch Mt.** (898 m), which provides fine views of the southern part of the region of Spiš and the northern Gemer. Continue from the saddle turning left onto the red-marked (0901) Cesta hrdinov SNP road (E8). Still ascending in undulated terrain along the ridge of the Volovské vrchy Mts. pass through the forest, clearings and meadows with wonderful views. Reaching the **Smrečinka** crossroads (1,225 m) turn left and the marking of the path changes from red to yellow (8746) now heading to the north. Still ascending you will arrive at the top of the **Babiná Mt.** (1,278 m), the highest point of our trip. Then comes a steep descent from the top. In half way of the descent is a short traverse to the right on narrow asphalt road. Shortly after you will have to turn left downwards and continue along the brook to the little village of **Sykavka** (690 m) in the Hnilecká dolina valley, which also is part of Mlynky. Continue to the left on yellow mark walking comfortably on a narrow asphalt road. Walking along the river of Hnilec you will get to the village of Rakovec. The route runs on the grassy bottom of the valley between forested slopes. Advance along the railway track. Continue from Rakovec shortly on the green mark, like at the beginning of the trip, which ends in the village of **Mlynky**.

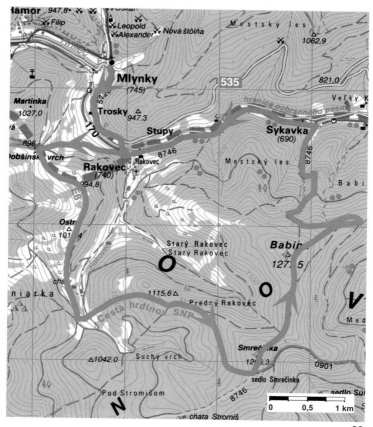

26 The Veľká Knola Mt.

Novoveská Huta – Čertova hlava – Pod Muráňom – Veľká Knola – Malá Knola – Grajnár – Gretla – Novoveská Huta

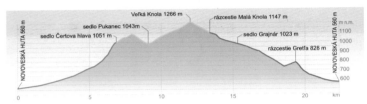

Situation: The Volovské vrchy Mts. - West
Starting and finishing point: Novoveská Huta, bus stop, parking lot.
Time schedule: Novoveská Huta - Čertova hlava 2 h - Pod Muráňom ¾ h - Veľká Knola ½ h - Malá Knola ¼ h - Grajnár ½ h

- Gretla 1 ¼ h - Novoveská Huta ¾ h.
Total: 6 hours.
Elevation gain: 676 m.
Map: Volovské vrchy - Krompachy 1 : 50 000 (sheet 125), VKÚ, š. p., Harmanec.

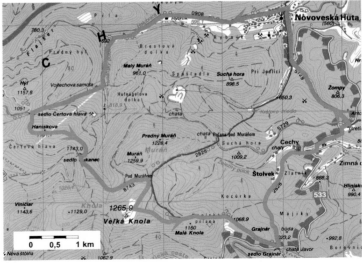

Classification: Moderately difficult circle. It runs on quality forest roads and paths. The stretch around Novoveská Huta and Gretla runs along the state road. Orientation is easy thanks to good marking. Pay attention to the changing colour of marking.

Basic route: You will ascend to the wide mountain top included in the Protected Area of Knola. Conservationists focus their attention to the rare wood species and fowl living in these parts. Passing through the locality Rybník the trail leads in the forest and approaches small water reservoir at the locality of Vojtechová samota. Later is runs over the grassy ridge of Malá Knola and the saddle of Grajnár before it descends again to Novoveská Huta.

Start at **Novoveská Huta** (560 m), part of the town of Spišská Nová Ves. It heads to the west following the red mark (0908). It crosses the nice valley of the Holubnica brook and continues slightly up on narrow asphalt road on the edge of an open valley. Pass by the group of houses at Rybník and continue south-westward in the forest. Later you will have to turn left up the red-marked trail to Vojtechova samota. Pass by a small water reservoir and carry on steep forest road up to the **Čertova hlava** saddle (1,051 m). Having a short rest at this attractive place continue to the left on the yellow mark (8743) up the forest path. Later comes the traverse below the Haniskova Mt. and the descent down to the saddle of Pukanec (1,143 m). Continue ascending on the yellow-marked forest road as far as the **Pod Muráňom** crossroads (1,181 m). It is only several tens of meters long ascent, which leads to half-forested top of the **Veľká Knola** Mt. (1,266 m), the highest point of the trip. It is worth the toil. You can admire the far-reaching views of the mountainous landscape surrounding this part of the Volovské vrchy Mts. Descend down the forest to the **Malá Knola** crossroads (1,147 m) and later in easier terrain down the blue-marked (2828) trail running in meadows and forest as far as the Grajnár saddle (1,023 m). There is a road at the saddle connecting the regions of Spiš and Gemer and your blue-marked path runs parallel to the road for a while. Continue down the forest following the blue mark and later pass through the alpine meadow of Štolvek. You are now drawing closer to the western edge of the village of Hnilčík and the trail leads shortly on asphalt road in the upper part of this village. Later it enters the forest, passes by a cross next to the state road and drops down to the **Gretla** crossroads (828 m). Turn here onto the green-marked trail (5729) to continue down the forest road as far as the **Novoveská Huta.** The final part of the your trail runs together with the blue-marked hiking path along the state road to the centre of the suburb and the bus stop.

27 The Pálenica Mt.

Teplička – Gretla – Grajnár – Pálenica – Hnilčík – Bindt – Teplička

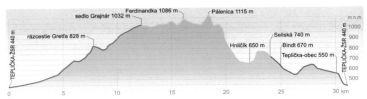

Situation: The Volovské vrchy Mts. - West
Starting and finishing point: Teplička, bus stop, railway station, parking lot.
Time schedule: Teplička - Gretla 2 ½ h - Grajnár 1 ¼ h - Pálenica 1 ½ h - Hnilčík-Mraznica 1 h - Hnilčík ¼ h - Seliská ¾ h

- Labková ¼ h - Bindt ¼ h - Teplička 1 h.
Total: 8 ¾ hours.
Elevation gain: 675 m.
Map: Volovské vrchy - Krompachy 1 : 50 000 (sheet 125), VKÚ, š. p., Harmanec.

Classification: Difficult trip for its length. It runs mostly on forest roads. Orientation is easy thanks to good marking.
Basic route: The route leads in less visited part of the Volovské vrchy Mts. The stretch between Gretla and Grajnár saddle is an exception as it comes near to the state road. It is an exacting but also very attractive and peaceful outing.

The trip starts at the village of **Teplička** (465 m). It heads to the southwest following the blue mark from the railway station at the edge of the village. The first stretch is a long walk through the valley of the Teplický Brusník brook on narrow asphalt road mostly through the forest. You are passing by the mining buildings and continue in the forest. At the end of the stretch is a steep ascent as far as the state road to the Gretla crossroads (828 m). Sticking to the blue mark walk along the road until you reach a cross where you turn left and downward. Pass through the upper part of the village of Hnilčík and return back to the forest road. Ascend to the saddle of Grajnár (1,022 m). Continue from the saddle following the yellow mark (8744). Cross the state road and enter the forest and walk on the path, the first part of which is marked in yellow and green and later the comfortable forest road is marked only in yellow. Ascend and walk alternatively in the forest and meadows as far as **Pálenica Mt.** (1,115 m), the highest point of the trip. You will forget the toil as soon as you reach the top of Pálenica Mt. as it opens attractive views of the Volovské vrchy Mts. Descend from Pálenica Mt. in meadows and forest to the ski resort Hnilčík-Mraznica. You will reach the narrow valley of the Zelený potok brook and continue on asphalt road to the **Hnilčík** crossroads (635 m). If you want to have a rest, the village of Hnilčík is the best place. After having some refreshment continue on the yellow marked road (8744), which ascends from the confluence of brooks to the open grassy crest with the crossroads of **Seliská** (740 m). It turns left there and after a while you will find yourself at the **Labková** crossroads (720 m). Turn right at the crossroads onto the green mark (5750) and continue through the Hnilecké vrchy Mts. and return through the old mining village of **Bindt** (670 m) going to the north. After descending from Bindt continue in undulated terrain through the forest and meadows and the trip ends in the village of **Teplička**.

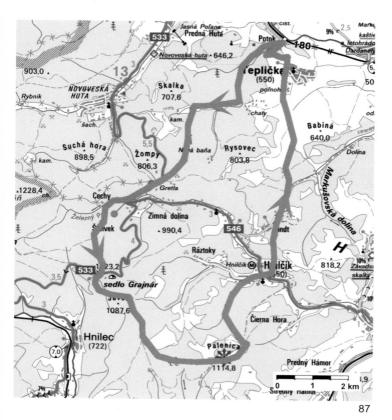

28 Southern ridge of the Hnilecké vrchy Mts.

Hnilčík – Žaloba – Závadka – Pod Holým vrchom – Poráč

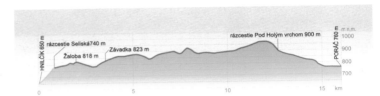

Situation: The Hnilecké vrchy Mts.
Starting point: Hnilčík, bus stop, parking lot.
Finishing point: Poráč, bus stop, parking lot.
Time schedule: Hnilčík - Seliská ¾ h -
Žaloba ¾ h - Smrečina ¾ h - Rovná lúka
1 h - Pod Holým vrchom ¾ h - Poráč ¾ h.
Total: 4 ¾ hours. **Elevation gain:** 250 m.
Map: Volovské vrchy - Krompachy
1 : 50 000 (sheet 125), VKÚ, š. p., Harmanec.

Classification: Moderately difficult tour. Only the initial ascent to the crest of the Hnilecké vrchy Mts. from Hnilčík requires a bit of strain. The rest of the trail runs in moderately undulated terrain. It leads on well-marked forest roads and paths. Orientation can become difficult in case of bad weather.
Basic route: This attractive trip will introduce the hiker to great part of the open grassy crest of the southern part of the Hnilecké vrchy Mts. It offers far-reaching panoramic views of the dissected landscape of the region of Spiš. The Vysoké Tatry Mts. can be seen in the north-west, while the Levočské vrchy and the main ridge of the Volovské vrchy Mts. are in the north and south respectively. Original folk architecture can be admired in the typical villages of Závadka and Poráč.

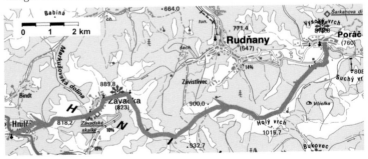

Hnilecké vrchy Mts. from Závadka

The route starts in the central part of the village of **Hnilčík** (650 m). The yellow mark (8744) leads from the crossroads of the state road to the northeast. Pass several meters along the road and turn left towards the confluence of the Ráztoka and Železný potok brooks. Continue on the path traversing the slope of the valley of the Železný potok brook. Walking in half open terrain and later in forest you will come to the wide half-forested ridge with the **Seliská** crossroads (740 m) Turn right following the green mark (5750). Now you walk comfortable on the edge of the forest, later slightly up the slope and through the meadows of Žaloba. You can enjoy fine views of the Spiš region, which will accompany you along the whole stretch of the route. Pass by a wooden cross at the forest edge and continue as far as the lower end of the village of **Závadka** (823 m). Turning slightly to the left walk up the village and later on field road you will ascend onto a wide grassy ridge. Pass by a chapel and comfortable path will carry you through the meadows to the forested part of the ridge and road post of **Smrečina** (840 m). Reaching the crossroads turn left and continue following the green mark. In the following part of the route is a moderate ascent in the forest and meadows before you reach a sheep farm on the crest. Continue in open terrain traversing the northern slope of the crest. Shortly after you will come to the **Pod Holým vrchom** crossroads (900 m), which is the highest point of the trip. Turn left onto the blue-marked path (2827). Descend in forest and alpine meadow called Svinský hřbok as far as an open saddle coming the state road. Continue to the right along the road. Then you will comfortably descend to the village of **Poráč** (760 m).

29 The Volovec Mt.

Hnilec – Súľová – Peklisko – Čertova hoľa – Volovec – Skalisko – Volovec – Henclová

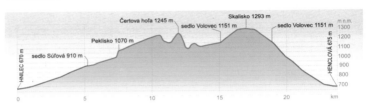

Situation: The Volovské vrchy Mts.

Starting point: Hnilec, bus stop, railway station, parking lot.

Finishing point: Henclová, bus stop, parking lot.

Time schedule: Hnilec - Súľová 1 h - Peklisko ¾ h - Čertova hoľa 1 ¼ h - Volovec ½ h - Skalisko ½ h - Volovec ¼ h - Henclová 1 ¼ h.

Total: 5 ½ hours.

Elevation gain: 633 m.

Map: Volovské vrchy - Krompachy 1 : 50 000 (sheet 125), VKÚ, š. p., Harmanec.

Classification: Moderately difficult tour for its length and altitude difference. It runs mostly on forest roads and paths. Thanks to good marking orientation is easy. The stretch between Hnilec and the Súľová saddle requires concentration as it lacks marking and its runs along a not too frequented state road.

Basic route: It is a rather demanding passage through the western part of the main ridge of the Volovské vrchy Mts., which forms the bulkiest group of the tops. One of its northern side ridges includes the tallest peak of the mountain range, Zlatý stôl Mt. Option to this trip is the ascent to its top.

The trip starts in **Hnilec** (722 m). It heads to the south along unmarked state road in the direction of Rožňava. Then comes the moderate ascent to the saddle of **Súľová** (910 m). Continue on the red-marked (0901) Cesta hrdinov SNP road (E8). Turn left at the saddle and walk shortly along the road. Turn left onto the forest road after a while. Ascend first below the ridge then on up the ridge. Then there is the steep ascent to the **Peklisko** Mt. (1,070 m). Continue ascending first on forest road, later on a path below the Hoľa Mt. Undulated terrain follows before you reach the top of the **Čertova hoľa** Mt. (1,245 m). Then the route turns to the south though it sticks to the red-marked path. Walk in the undulated terrain immediately below the ridge as far as the grassy saddle towards the **Volovec** crossroads (1,151 m). Then continue following the red mark and ascend the denuded **Volovec Mt.**

(1,284 m) and further on the **Skalisko** cliff (1,293 m). The strain invested will be rewarded by far-reaching views of the mountainous eastern part of Slovakia. A wonderful panoramic view of the southern part of the regions of Spiš and northern part of Gemer opens once you reach the highest point of the trip, the top of the cliff of Skalisko. The top group of cliffs is part of the peak of Volovec. Return back to the Volovec saddle by the same way. Turn right at the saddle and continue descending down the green-marked trail (5720). Now you are descending down the northern slope of the Volovec Mt.

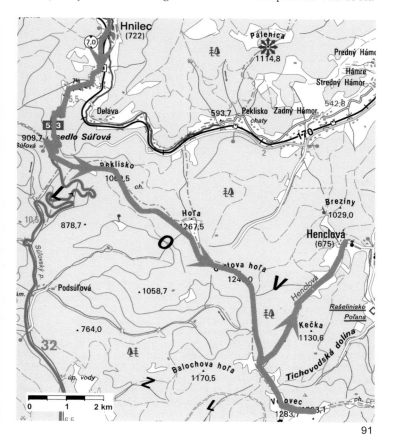

Henclová

on forest roads and paths, which repeatedly cross the Henclová brook. Later continue along the brook and enter the open grassy part of the little valley. The path crossing it will carry you to the former mining village of **Henclová** (675 m), which apart from offering refreshment boasts examples of the original folk architecture and a wonderful natural setting.

Option: Demanding and especially fit hikers can continue from the Volovec Mt. walking on top of the ridge following the red mark (0901) as far as the crossroads called sedlo Krivé. Turning left and sticking to the blue mark he can ascend to the tallest peak of the Volovské vrchy Mts., **Zlatý stôl** (1,322 m). The descent follows the blue mark to the village of Stará Voda and from there it is possible to continue on the blue mark to the village of Švedlár where there are bus stop and railway station. Total time: eight and a half hours.

30 From Henclová to Nálepkovo

Henclová – Zahájnica – Pod Streleckým vrchom – Nálepkovo

Situation: The Volovské vrchy Mts.
Starting point: Henclová, bus stop, parking lot.
Finishing point: Nálepkovo, bus stop, railway station, parking lot.
Time schedule: Henclová - Zahájnica ½ h - Pod Streleckým vrchom ¾ h - Nálepkovo ¾ h.
Total: 2 hours. **Elevation gain:** 137 m.
Map: Volovské vrchy - Krompachy 1 : 50 000 (sheet 125), VKÚ, š. p., Harmanec.

Classification: Easy tour. Its first and last stretches lead on asphalt road with scarce traffic. The rest is a little demanding passage across the ridge on forest road. Pay attention when descending from the foothill to the Hnilecká dolina valley as the marking is not especially good there. Orientation is easy as the major part of the trail is well-marked.

Basic route: The route offers a comfortable passage through the little visited part of the Volovské vrchy Mts.

It starts at the old mining village of **Henclová** (675 m) hidden below the northern slopes of the Volovec Mt. The village is attractive for its typical folk architecture. Green-marked path (5720) connects the village with the main ridge of the Volovské vrchy Mts. But our route leads in the opposite direction on the green-marked path heading to the north and northeast. It descends down the narrow valley of the Henclová brook with forested slopes. Walk along asphalt road with scarce traffic in "company" of the Tichá voda brook. When the valley widens continue on its grassy bottom and pass through the village of **Zahájnica**, part of the village of Nálepkovo. About 200 m beyond the bus stop turn left off the road and leave the valley walking among the last houses. Continue on the green-marked trail shortly down over the brook and pass onto the forest road. Ascend to

93

Nálepkovo

the right up to the ridge, which inclines to the northeastern aspect of the main ridge of the Volovské vrchy Mts. and separates the Tichovodská dolina valley from the Hnilecká dolina valley. Once you reach the crossroads of the forest roads in the saddle turn right and go down the forest. After comfortable and little demanding passage through the forested ridge you will reach the Hnilecká dolina valley. This nice valley with wide grassy bottom and slopes is adorned by forest reaching as far as the ridge. Descend bellow the **Strelecký vrch Mt.** into the open Hnilecká dolina valley onto asphalt road. Walk along the railway track towards the village of **Nálepkovo** (538 m). Passing the railway underpass you will come to the village. Turn right at the crossroads next to the Železný potok brook. Walk along the brook for a while then turn left and cross the footbridge. Continue up to the state road and shortly after you reach the railway station, which means the end of this comfortable trip.

31 The Bukovec Mt.

Švedlár – Bukovec – Pod Holým vrchom – Poráč

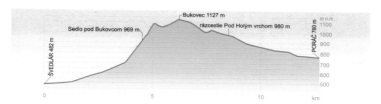

Situation: The Volovské vrchy Mts., south of Spiš.
Starting point: Švedlár, bus stop, railway station, parking lot.
Finishing point: Poráč, bus stop, parking lot.
Time schedule: Švedlár - Sedlo pod Bukovcom 1 ¼ h - Bukovec ¾ h - Pod Holým vrchom ½ h - Poráč ¾ h.
Total: 3 ¼ hours.
Elevation gain: 645 m.
Map: Volovské vrchy – Krompachy 1 : 50 000 (sheet 125), VKÚ, š. p., Harmanec.

Classification: Medium difficult tour thanks to the considerable altitude difference. The route is on quality roads and paths. Orientation becomes a bit complicated in open terrain along the descent from Bukovec, but on the other side good marking is of great help.
Basic route: It leads in the scarcely visited part of the Volovské vrchy Mts. But the natural setting of the deep coniferous forests is attractive and above all quite and almost intact. Forested crest of the Hnilické vrchy Mts. alternates with open meadows. They, like the top of the Bukovec Mt., offer fine views of great part of the region of Spiš. The whole route sticks to the blue-marked hiking path (2827).

It starts at the railway station of **Švedlár** (482 m) and turns left on the state road through the village. The views of the deforested round top of the Bukovec Mt. suddenly open in front of you. Abandoning the meadow the road moderately ascends following the brook. At the point where the forest road leaves the brook behind a steeper ascent starts. First you are walking in the forest later you will find yourself on a meadow with a hunter's stand and a fine view of the Hnilecké vrchy Mts. The route turns to the right up the forest. After about 500 m turn left and a short ascent leads to the crest and the crossroads of **Sedlo pod Bukovcom** (969 m). Continue to the left up the forested crest where the green-marked hiking path (5750) joins your route. Later you will arrive at the open and grassy crest, which will carry you to the top of the **Bukovec Mt.** (1,127 m). As you are ascending gradually

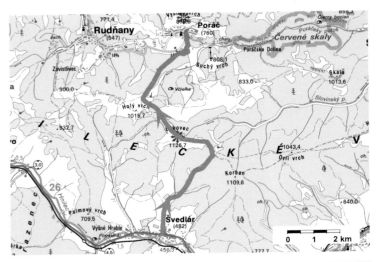

96

the views first of Švedlár in the winding Hnilecká dolina valley and then the surrounding mountain ranges open. The view you get from the top of the Bukovec is worth the toil. The descent from the top, which coincides with blue and green marks, is first moderate then it becomes steeper and it runs in the forest. After a while you have to turn right and downward. Electric posts also indicate the route of the return trip. Continue traversing the meadow in the direction of transformer and take the forest road at your left. A short traverse follows and it will carry you to the **Pod Holým vrchom** crossroads (980 m). Leave now the green mark and continue to the right and down following the blue mark. First you walk in the forest and later across the meadow called Svinský hŕbok as far as the state road connecting Rudňany and Poráč. Turn right and walking along the road you will get to the village of **Poráč** (760 m) with opportunity to buy some refreshment there. This is where the route ends.

Option: You can make the trip longer, if you continue on the crest from the Pod Holým vrchom crossroads following the green mark (5750) as far as the mountain village of Závadka, which has bus connection with Nálepkovo. The overall duration of the trip will be then 4 and three quarters of an hour.

The panorama of Švedlár

32 The Galmus plateau

Poráč – Zbojský stôl – Nad Sejkovou – Galmus – Pod Skalou – Krompachy

Situation: The Hnilecké vrchy Mts.
Starting point: Poráč, bus stop, parking lot.
Finishing point: Krompachy, bus stop, railway station, parking lot.
Time schedule: Poráč - Zbojský stôl ¾ h

- Nad Sejkovou ¾ h - Galmus ¾ h - Pod Skalou ½ h - Krompachy ¾ h.
Total: 3 ½ hours. **Elevation gain:** 491 m.
Map: Volovské vrchy - Krompachy 1 : 50 000 .(sheet 125), VKÚ, š. p., Harmanec.

Classification: Easy trip in undulated terrain. Only the long descent from the Galmus plateau to Krompachy is a bit demanding. The trail leads on forest roads and paths and it is well-marked. Though the altitude difference is relatively large, the route mostly descends and heads to its lowest point in Krompachy
Basic route: This comfortable route makes possible to see the northern part of the Hnilecké vrchy Mts. It ascends from the grassy setting around the typical village of Poráč to the forested ridge. The views of the southern ridge of the Hnilecké vrchy from Bukovec to the Krompašský vrch Mt. and the Hornádska kotlina basin in the north make the trip more attractive. The final part of the route passes through the attractive setting of the karstic plateau of Galmus. The sinkholes in this locality are interesting.

The route starts at the village of **Poráč** (760 m) and follows the blue hiking mark (2827) heading to the north-east. First it passes through mountain meadows with nice view of the Poráčska dolina valley and the environs of the Hnilecké vrchy. The dominant of the southern view is the tallest mountain of **Bukovec** (1,127 m). Continue slightly ascending, later pass through the

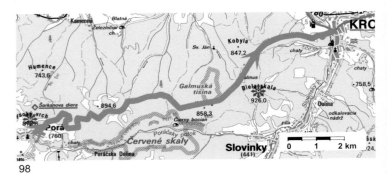

Valley of the Hnilec

forest to a meadow before you reach the road post of **Zbojský stôl**. Continue ascending to the highest point of the route. Then descend in undulated forest terrain to the road post of **Nad Sajkovou**. Continue descending in mixed forest and cross the meadow with sinkholes. Now you enter the forest and passing through it you will arrive at the **Galmus** crossroads (740 m). Turn right and ascend to half-forested terrain. Later you will have to pass through another meadow with sinkholes and continue as far as the edge of the plateau. Continuous mild descent on forest road and around the **Pod Skalou** road post (610 m) starts here. Now you are walking on an open ridge with captivating views of the mountainous setting around Krompachy and the Hornád valley. Pass by the bus station to the **Krompachy** crossroads (379 m). Continue to the left following the yellow mark (8771) as far as the railway station where this comfortable trip ends.

Option A: You can make the trip longer (by about an hour, including the return trip) and more attractive by ascent to the top of the **Biela skala** (926 m). Turn right up the blue-marked trail at the Galmus crossroads. The blue mark joins here the green instructive path. Return by the same way to the Galmus crossroads.

Option B: You can also descend from the top of the Biela skala to Krompachy taking the green-marked trail. The total time of the route from Poráč to Krompachy will be four hours then.

33 The recreation resort of Plejsy

Krompachy – Plejsy – Krompašský vrch – Slovinky

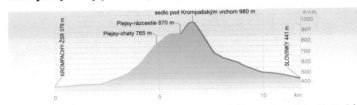

Situation: The Hnilecké vrchy Mts.

Starting point: Krompachy, bus stop, railway station, parking lot.

Finishing point: Slovinky, bus stop, parking lot.

Time schedule: Krompachy - Plejsy-chaty 1 ½ h - Plejsy ¼ h - sedlo pod Krompašským vrchom ¼ h - Rošty 1 h - Slovinky 1 h.

Total: 4 hours.

Elevation gain: 601 m.

Map: Volovské vrchy - Krompachy 1 : 50 000 (sheet 125), VKÚ, š. p., Harmanec.

Classification: Moderately difficult tour. The initial part consisting of long ascent from Krompachy to the ridge of the Hnilecké vrchy Mts. when in two hours the altitude difference of 601 m must be overcome is difficult. Almost the whole route is on quality forest roads and orientation is easy thanks to good marking.

Basic route: This nice tour offers numerous views of the mountainous setting of the Hnilecké vrchy Mts. and the head of the Hornádska kotlina basin below the Branisko Mts. It ascends to the much sought after ski resort of Plejsy. It shortly passes through the southern part of the ridge of the Hnilecké vrchy Mts. and eventually heads to the attractive environment of the village of Slovinky.

The trip starts at the railway station of **Krompachy** (379 m) and shortly follows the yellow mark (8771) to the town and the crossroads. Continue following the green mark (5750), which leads together with the yellow mark through

Plejsy

the town. At the southern edge of the town the green-mark trail ascends to the meadows followed by the forest. The ascent in forest is steep and later when you approach to the first recreation buildings at the ski centre of Plejsy it becomes milder. Traverse across the ski track to the **Plejsy-chaty** crossroads (765 m). Continue on the green mark, which joins here the blue and yellow marks. Ascend up the ski track around the mountain hotel. Then the path becomes milder and if you continue up the forest road you will reach the **Plejsy** crossroads (870 m). The red mark joins your trail and you continue to the right along with the blue and green marked trails. The passage over the ridge sporadically offers fine views of the environs. Reaching the highest point of the route, the crossroads in the saddle **Pod Krompašským vrchom** (980 m) continue on the red-marked trail gradually leaving the blue and green marks. Descend first to the right down from the ridge in undulated terrain. Then the descent down the forested road becomes steeper and milder closely before you reach the **Rošty** crossroads with fine view of the Slovinky village. Continue descending down the open terrain and in the forest as far as the mining plant in **Slovinky** (441 m). When you reach the state road turn right and walk up the village to the municipal office, where the trip ends.

34 Passage through the Poráčska dolina valley

Slovinky – Poráčska dolina – Čierny bocian – Poráč

Situation: The Volovské vrchy Mts., south of Spiš.
Starting point: Slovinky, bus stop, parking lot.
Finishing point: Poráč, bus stop, parking lot.

Time schedule: Slovinky - Čierny bocian ¾ h - Poráčska Dolina 1 ¼ h - Poráč ½ h.
Total: 2 ½ hours. **Elevation gain:** 319 m.
Map: Volovské vrchy – Krompachy 1 : 50 000 (sheet 125), VKÚ, š. p., Harmanec.

Classification: Easy and comfortable tour on good roads, easy orientation. Refreshment available at the cottage of Čierny bocian.
Basic route: A rewarding easy trip in the quite environment of the northern part of the Volovské vrchy Mts. or as they are sometimes referred to the Hnilecké vrchy Mts. The Poráčska dolina valley is deeply incised in sometimes continuos karstic plateau of Galmus. The steep limestone faces in its central part called the Červené skaly rocks are the National Nature Reserve. It is the most valuable territory of the kind in the Volovské vrchy Mts.

The route starts at the crossroads of the village of **Slovinky** (441 m). The red-marked route (0916) heads westward. The narrow asphalt road you are walking on at the beginning leads as far as the Čierny bocian cottage. On your left you can see the top of the Skala Mt. (1,014 m). It lies on the grassy plateau of Slovinská skala. The larger part of the route leads along the Poráčsky jarok brook. Coming out of the village the route first passes through meadow and later in forest before you reach the **Čierny bocian** cottage. Continue along the brook on a forest road while you pass through the narrowest part of the valley. The recreation settlement of **Poráčska dolina** follows. It is situated in the open and widened part of the eponymous valley. Then you arrive at the **Poráčska dolina-chaty** crossroads. The route leads on narrow asphalt road, which will bring you to the final ascent to the village of **Poráč** (760 m). On your right side is a recreation establishment and on your left is a ski lift. While waiting for the bus you can have some refreshment or you can shortly ascend to the top of the **Vysoký vrch Mt.** (874 m).

Valley of Slovinky from Plejsy

It is worth the toil although no path leads to the top, as is offers a complete view of the environs. You can return by the same way to the village or you can descend to the cave of Šarkanova diera lying on the opposite slope.

Option: You can abandon the track next to the cottage Čierny bocian and use the green-marked path to ascend to the right up the northern slope to the plateau of Galmus. Joining the route No. 32 and following the blue mark (2827) you can then continue to Poráč (the total time of the trip is then four hours) or to Krompachy (total time three and half hours).

35 The Sľubica Mt.

Krompachy – Kaľava – Vojkovce – Sľubica – Dúbrava

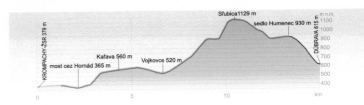

Situation: The Branisko Mts.
Starting point: Krompachy, bus stop, railway station, parking lot.
Finishing point: Dúbrava, bus stop, parking lot.
Time schedule: Krompachy - Kaľava

1 ¼ h - Vojkovce ¾ h - Sľubica 1 ¼ h - Dúbrava 1 ¼ h. **Total:** 4 ½ hours.
Elevation gain: 750 m.
Map: Volovské vrchy - Krompachy 1 : 50 000 (sheet 125), VKÚ, š. p., Harmanec.

Classification: Difficult tour. Steep ascent from Vojkovce to the Sľubica Mt. is followed by the demanding descent from the top to the saddle of Humenec. The route leads mostly on forest roads. It is well-marked with the exception of the stretch between Krompachy and Kaľava.
Basic route: You will have the opportunity to admire the landscape of the eastern edge of the Hornádska kotlina basin. First you will ascend to the mountain villages of Kaľava and Vojkovce and then to the top of the Sľubica Mt. The terrain opens sporadically and offers nice views of the Hornádska kotlina basin and the surrounding mountain ranges.

Start at the railway station of **Krompachy** (379 m) following the yellow-mark on the road heading to the west. Turn right at the first crossroads onto the green mark (5704). Continue ahead along industrial buildings heading to the north out of the town. Walk on the embankment by the water reservoir on a path until you get close to the railway track. Take the sharp turn to the right and continue up by an isolated building. Soon you will pass through a meadow and enter a thin forest. The steep ascent ends on the meadow near the village of **Kaľava** (560 m). Pass by the electric line and around a cross and soon after you will find yourself directly at the centre of the village. Continue comfortably on a narrow asphalt road heading to the village of **Vojkovce** (520 m). When you reach the local church turn right onto the forest road. Mild ascent along the brook out of the village follows. Then there is steeper ascent in the forest, which ends next to the draining channel marked in yellow (8731). Continue together with the yellow mark slightly upwards across a small meadow to the forest. Soon after you will have to turn left off the forest road onto a steep path. At the final stretch of the ascent is a moderate ascent to the top of the **Sľubica Mt.** (1,129 m), the highest point of this route. Demanding ascent to the most southernmost top of the Branisko mountain range offers far-reaching views of wonderful sceneries of the dissected relief of the southern part of Spiš. After a short rest at the top continue on the green-marked path to the north. The trail lead on the ridge of the Branisko mountain range separating the historical regions of Spiš and Šariš. A moderate descent follows and shortly after you will arrive at the crossroads of your path with forest road. Stick to the green mark and you will pass by a sheep farm. The route leads first to the north then it drops to the western side with the saddle of **Humenec** (930 m). Turn left there to the unmarked forest road and continue descending westward below the National Nature Reserve of Rajtopiky. In a while you will find yourself at the village of **Dúbrava** (615 m) where the trip ends.

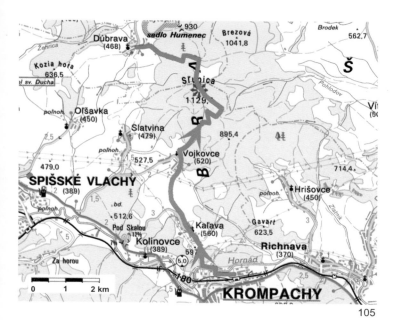

36 The Markušovský skalný hríb rock

Matejovce – Markušovský skalný hríb – Markušovce

Situation: The Hornádska kotlina basin.
Starting point: Matejovce, bus stop, railway station, parking lot.
Finishing point: Markušovce, bus stop, railway station, parking lot.
Time schedule: Matejovce - Markušov-

ský skalný hríb ¾ h - Markušovce ¾ h.
Total: 1 ½ hours.
Elevation gain: 10 m.
Map: Volovské vrchy - Krompachy 1 : 50 000 (sheet 125), VKÚ, š. p., Harmanec.

Classification: Easy tour free from any pronounced ascents. It leads on forest path and through meadows. Orientation is easy.
Basic route: The whole walk is marked in yellow. It passes on the edge of the Hornád basin. The meandering river Hornád will accompany you the whole time. Inconspicuous slopes covered by pines skirt the northern side of the route. It contains the national nature phenomenon of Markušovské skaly rocks, a large Flysch face with several mushroom-shaped rock formations. The Markušovský skalný hríb rock (The Stone Mushroom of Markušovce) is the largest of them.

The route starts at the railway station of **Matejovce** (427 m). It follows the yellow hiking mark (8763) first shortly to the north on field road. Cross the bridge over the Hornád and leave the field road at the end of the forest. Continue to the left onto the forest path heading to the west. Pass by the Kamenný obrázok, which is the reminder of the 1817 flood when the water level of the Hornád river reached extreme values. Continue on the edge of the forest until you come to the unique natural form called **Markušovský skalný hríb** (The Stone Mushroom of Markušovce, 409 m). It is 8 m tall rock

formation similar to mushroom, which originated in the consequence of irregular weathering of rocks. The path approaches the rock. Continue on the forest edge and the Hornád river is always near. Later you will walk over the meadows as far as the edge of **Markušovce** (440 m). Walk along the river and later cross the bridge to the right bank of the river and the state road. Then you can continue either to the left and you will end at the railway station or you can turn right, arrive at the bus stop at the centre of the village and have

Markušovský skalný hríb rock

an opportunity to see the local landmarks including the manor house with exposition of furniture. You can also visit the summer castle of Dardanely with exposition of musical instruments.

37 The Spiš Castle (Spišský hrad)

Sivá Brada – Spišská Kapitula – Spišské Podhradie – Spišský hrad – Dreveník – Žehra

Situation: The Hornádska kotlina basin.
Starting point: Sivá Brada, parking lot.
Finishing point: Žehra, bus stop, parking lot.
Time schedule: Sivá Brada - Jazierko na pažiti ¾ h - Spišské Podhradie ½ h -
Spišský hrad ½ h - Dreveník ½ h - Žehra 1 h.
Total: 3 ¼ hours. **Elevation gain:** 174 m.
Map: Volovské vrchy - Krompachy 1 : 50 000 (sheet 125), VKÚ, š. p., Harmanec.

Classification: Easy tour in slightly undulated terrain. Only the ascent to the Spiš Castle requires a bit of strain. Thanks to the views that accompany the hiker for the whole of the trip and good marking, there are no problems with orientation. The trail is also an instructive path.
Basic route: The route coincides with the favourite instructive path attractive for its rare combination of cultural and natural assets concentrated on the small territory of Spiš. It runs in the picturesque landscape of Podbranisko at the north-eastern tip of the Hornádska kotlina basin. Its main dominant is the Spiš Castle.

The route starts at the **Sivá Brada** (480 m) below the roadhouse of Spišský salaš. It follows the yellow hiking mark (8768) parallel to the instructive path Sivá Brada-Dreveník. Initially it passes through the Nature Reserve of Sivá Brada, the youngest travertine hill. It runs shortly over the road as far as the parking lot to accessible mineral springs. You can observe the origin of travertine under the effect of the emanating mineral water. On a hill above the spring is a pilgrim chapel. The route passes by and along the state road. Then it turns to the left and passes by recreation building. Passing through the field you will arrive at what is called Kamenný obrázok and among islands of pine trees you will ascend to the travertine hill **Jazierko na Pažiti**. This little intermittent lake with non-periodic activity is a much-appreciated natural phenomenon. Continue comfortably through the meadows with the view

The Spiš Castle and Spišské Podhradie

of the Spiš Chapter and Spiš Castle. Soon after you will cross the road and arrive at the former Church town of **Spišská Kapitula**, now the town reserve. You should not miss it and see especially its Late Romanesque cathedral. Continue down to **Spišské Podhradie** (435 m). At the end of the little town before you arrive at the railway station turn left off the road. Ascend up the meadows to the travertine hill of **Spišský hradný vrch** (634 m) with the dominating Natural Cultural Monument of Spiš Castle. The castle is one of the largest castle complexes in ruins in Central Europe and its visit will certainly intrigue every visitor. It also contains exhibition of arms. Continue from the parking lot below the castle following the yellow mark over the travertine hill of Ostrá hora. Now you are drawing closer to the most extensive travertine formation in Slovakia, the National Reserve of **Dreveník**. This rock town with several karst forms is very interesting. Ascend by the rock towers to a conspicuous travertine plateau with nice views. Return going down the meadow and you will come to the nearest village of **Hodkovce** (480 m). Pass by the manor house and continue to the right along the state road, which will carry you to the next village, which is **Žehra** (440 m). The local Church of the Holy Spirit with precious medieval wall paintings is along with the Spiš Castle, Spišské Podhradie, Spišská Kapitula and Dreveník included in the UNESCO List of the World Cultural and Natural Heritage from 1993.

38 Around Levoča

Levoča – Zbojnícka lúka – Uhlisko – Levočská dolina – Mariánska hora – Levoča

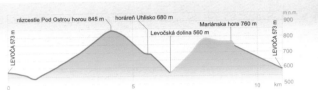

Situation: The Levočské vrchy Mts.
Starting and finishing point: Levoča, bus stop, parking lot.
Time schedule: Levoča - Zbojnícka lúka 1 ¾ h - Uhlisko ½ h - Levočská dolina ½ h

- Druhá lúka ¾ h - Mariánska hora ¼ h
- Levoča ½ h. **Total:** 4 ¼ hours.
Elevation gain: 272 m.
Map: Levočské vrchy 1 : 50 000 (sheet 114), VKÚ, š. p., Harmanec.

Classification: Moderately difficult circle leading mostly on forest roads and paths. The long ascent from Levoča to Ostrá hora Mt. and another steep ascent from the Levočská dolina valley to the Mariánska hora Mt. are the most demanding parts of this trip. Orientation is easy due to good marking.
Basic route: The tour introduces the hiker to a part of the mountainous Levočské úbočie hillside in the Levočské vrchy Mts. and the cultural monuments in the environs of Levoča. It provides nice views of the Hornádska kotlina basin and the chain of the Volovské vrchy Mts. It runs around the protected area of Uhliská and finally ascends to the dominant element in the environs of the town of Levoča: the pilgrim church of Visitation of the Virgin Mary at the Mariánska hora Mt.

The trip starts in **Levoča** (573 m) next to the Košická brána Gate. It follows the green hiking mark heading to the north-west. Walk down the town along the road to the Levočská dolina valley. Turn left over the Levočský

potok brook. After a short walk on asphalt road turn right onto field road. The road ascends through meadow and forest. Finally you will arrive at a clearing and the **Pod Ostrou horou** crossroads (845 m). This place offers fine views of Levoča and its environs. Continue to the right following the red mark. Go down alternatively through the forest and meadows. Pass by the protected lime trees above the gamekeeper's lodge **Uhlisko**. The lime growth and the game-

Levočské vrchy Mts.

keeper's lodge are apart of history connected with Štúr and his group, who pursued the Slovak national emancipating movement in the mid-19th century in this region. Continue descending to the **Levočská dolina** valley (560 m) towards the car camping side on the shore of the water reservoir. The place is ideal for relaxing especially in summer. Continue to the crossroads next to the state road and follow the yellow mark on the narrow asphalt road. After a while the yellow mark turns right and continues up a steep forest path. The ascent becomes milder close before you reach the **Druhá lúka** crossroads (775 m). Turn right there and walk comfortably on narrow asphalt road. The yellow and blue mark lead to the church of Visitation of the Virgin Mary at the **Mariánska hora Mt.** (760 m). It is also good opportunity to see the interior of the church and admire the view of Levoča and the surrounding mountain ranges. The return trip leads along the row of trees on asphalt road heading from the church to the road post of Mariánska hora-rázcestie. Continue then sticking to the blue marked down to the centre of the town of **Levoča**.

39 The ridge of the Levočské planiny plateaux

Levoča – Mariánska hora – Kúty – Uloža – Krúžok – Závada

Situation: The Levočské vrchy Mts.
Starting point: Levoča, bus stop, parking lot.
Finishing point: Závada, bus stop, parking lot.
Time schedule: Levoča - Mariánska hora

¾ h - Druhá lúka ¼ h - Kúty ¼ h - Zimná hôrka ¾ h - Uloža ¼ h - Krúžok ½ h - Závada ¾ h.
Total: 3 ½ hours. **Elevation gain:** 393 m.
Map: Levočské vrchy 1 : 50 000 (sheet 114), VKÚ, š. p., Harmanec.

Classification: Easy tour. Only the ascent to the Mariánska hora requires some increased efforts. The rest of the trip runs on comfortable terrain, mostly on well-marked forest roads.
Basic route: This is a comfortable tour along a part of the ridge of the Levočské planiny plains. It leads across the Mariánska hora Mt., passes through two mountain villages at the boundary of the Levočské úbočie hillslopes and Olšavická planina plateau. Almost the whole route offers numerous views of the mountainous landscape of the region of Spiš. Views of the dominating Vysoké Tatry Mts. in the west, the Hornádska kotlina basin skirted in the south by the Volovské vrchy Mts., Branisko Mts. and the Castle of Spiš in the south-east and the Levočské vrchy Mts. in the north gradually open in front of the hiker.

The trip starts in **Levoča** (573 m) next the Košická brána Gate. Follow the blue-mark heading to the north down the town. Then comes the ascent along the row of trees on asphalt path to the crossroads of Mariánska hora.

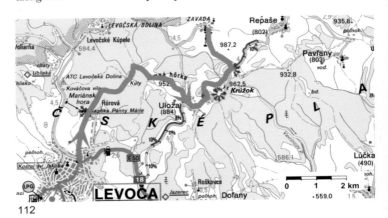

Levočské vrchy Mts.

Continue jointly with the yellow mark towards the church of Visitation of the Virgin Mary at the **Mariánska hora Mt.** (760 m). It is also good opportunity to see the interior of the church and admire Levoča and the surrounding mountain ranges. After this stop walk comfortable on asphalt road to the **Druhá lúka** crossroads (775 m). Abandon the yellow mark and continue following the blue mark shortly on asphalt road and soon after turn left up the path. Moderate ascent on forest road to unmistakable saddle with gamekeeper's lodge end at the crossroads of **Kúty** (830 m). Change to the red-marked path and turn right. Continue up the meadow edge, later through the forest and more meadows and you will arrive at the top of the **Zimná hôrka** Mt. (952 m). Descend to **Uloža** (884 m). Turn left on the state road and walk up the village. Next to the bus stop above the village turn off the state road to the left onto the forest road. Traverse the forest and meadows below the ridge as far as the **Krúžok** crossroads (966 m). This open flat top with thin forest growth also offers wonderful views. Leaving the highest point of the route behind continue following the yellow mark. Walk on the forest road, which turns to the north and descend comfortably through meadows and forest to draw closer to the village of **Závada** (820 m). The final stretch of the trip is the steep descent down the edge of the ski track to the village.

40 On the ridge of the Levočské úbočie

Hradisko – Brezová – Zbojnícka lúka – Levočská dolina – Kúty – Mariánska hora – Levoča

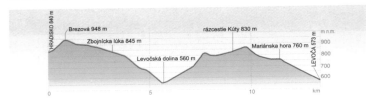

Situation: The Levočské vrchy Mts.

Starting point: Hradisko, bus stop, parking lot.

Finishing point: Levoča, bus stop, parking lot.

Time schedule: Hradisko - Brezová ½ h - Zbojnícka lúka 1 h - Uhlisko ½ h - Levočská dolina ½ h - Kúty 1 ¼ h - Druhá lúka ¼ h - Mariánska hora ¼ h - Levoča ½ h.

Total: 4 ¾ hours.

Elevation gain: 375 m.

Map: Levočské vrchy 1 : 50 000 (sheet 114), VKÚ, š. p., Harmanec.

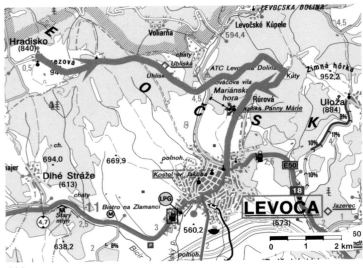

Classification: Moderately difficult trip. Short steep ascent to Brezová and the long ascent from the Levočská dolina valley to Kúty are the stretches requiring increased efforts. The rest of the trip is not demanding and it leads on forest roads and paths. The descent from the Mariánska hora Mt. to Levoča is on asphalt path. The route is well marked.

Basic route: This is the a trip to the scarcely visited southern part of the Levočské vrchy Mts. First you will pass on the open ridge of the Levočské úbočie hillslopes. Then the trail descends to the protected area of Uhliská. Later it passes through the grassy saddle of Kúty and continues to the Mariánska hora Mt. to the Visitation of the Virgin Mary church and ends in the historic town of Levoča.

Start at the village of **Hradisko** (840 m) eastward following the red mark. There is a short ascent to the top of the **Brezová Mt.** (948 m). It offers far-reaching views of the mountainous landscape of the southern and central parts of the region of Spiš with the dominating Vysoké Tatry Mts. in the west. Continue on the open ridge for about one kilometre on forest road jointly with the line of the main European water divide. A slight descent follows and then you have to pass through forest clearings to the **Pod Ostrou horou** crossroads (845 m). This stretch offers fine views of the environs. Continue following the red mark and descending down the forest and meadows to the gamekeeper's lodge of Uhlisko. The gamekeeper's lodge together with the contiguous area of protected lime trees are part of history connected with Štúr and his group, who pursued the Slovak national emancipating movement in the mid-19th century in this region Continue descending to the **Levočská dolina** valley (560 m) to the car camping site next to the water reservoir. The place is ideal for relaxing especially in summer. Short ascent together with yellow mark will carry you above the car-camping site. You will find yourself on a forest road and continue slightly ascending. Then the forest road changes into path and becomes steeper. When you get onto forest road again turn left and walk comfortably as far as grassy saddle with gamekeeper's lodge to the **Kúty** crossroads (830 m). The trail avoids the forested Burk mountain, continues to the right on the blue mark. Moderate descent on forest road and path leads to the **Druhá lúka** crossroads (755 m). Continue walking comfortably on narrow asphalt road. The blue mark and yellow mark lead to the church of Visitation of the Virgin Mary at the **Mariánska hora Mt.** (760 m). You can visit the church and see its interior while the top of the mountain also offers an interesting view of the town of **Levoča** (573 m). The town is an ideal final station of the trip as apart from numerous historical and cultural monuments it provides possibilities of refreshment and accommodation.

Natural landmarks and points of interests

The Slovenský raj Mts. – North

SPIŠSKÁ NOVÁ VES (470 m, population 39,000, route No. 1) and the villages west from the town are the starting points for the outings to Slovenský raj, an attractive area of karstic plateaus, gorges, waterfalls and caves with remarkable monuments and finding places of the traces of history.

SPIŠSKÉ TOMÁŠOVCE (532 m, population 1,400, route No. 2) is the best starting point for the north-eastern part of Slovenský raj. Not far away from Spišské Tomášovce is **Čingov** (494 m), the biggest tourist centre of Slovenský raj lying above the left bank of the Hornád (routes No. 3, 4, 5, 6). The Sovia skala rock located east from the village provides a fine view of Čingov and the Prielom Hornádu gorge (routes No. 2, 3).

Čingov lies in the lower part of **Prielom Hornádu** canyon (routes No. 4, 10, 11), one of the biggest tourist attraction of the Slovenský raj area. The narrow, canyon-like valley 16 kilometre long separated the marginal ridge culminating in **Tomášovský výhľad** view (667 m, routes No. 4, 5) from the mountain range. The ascent to the rock terrace facing south is worth the toil. The terrace provides a unique view of the lower part of the Prielom Hornádu canyon. In fine weather on the right side of the unique panorama also the curve of the High Tatra mountains is visible. The rock faces of the terrace are much sought out targets of the mountaineers. In 1889 the first private mountaineer shelter was built on the Tomášovský výhľad view. On the marginal crest closer to Čingov there are two nice rock formations called Ihla and Kazateľnica.

Through the lower stretch of the valley of the Hornád river leads a 15 kilometre long route of instructive path **Prielom Hornádu** with eleven information boards. Beyond the mouth of the Biely potok brook the path passes by the slope of Čertova sihoť Mt. (839 m) with the Čertova diera cave with scarce dripstone ornamentation but with abundant palaeontological and archaeological finds. Beyond the Letanovský mlyn the path goes back along the crest over the Tomášovský výhľad view to Čingov. Green-marked hiking route bends from the Prielom Hornádu gorge to the Tomášovská Belá valley. As one of the longest valleys in Slovenský raj area it starts below the karst plateau of Geravy, where the path intersects the national nature reserve **Holý kameň**, which protects the original forest communities including relic pines growing on limestone rock base. In the curve of the valley below Kláštorisko is the entrance to the gorge Kyseľ, unfortunately closed to the public at the present moment. The pride of the Kyseľ gorge is the Obrovský

Kláštorisko

vodopád waterfall, 60 metres tall. The tourists can enter the upper part of the gorge, which branches over the Karolinyho vodopád watefall (25 metres tall) to Vyšný, Malý and Veľký Kyseľ. Access is possible by the blue-marked trail starting in Kláštorisko. In Veľký Kyseľ the Pawlasov vodopád waterfall, bearing the name of the first victim the Slovenský raj area can be admired.

The **Sokolia dolina** valley joins the Tomášovská Belá valley in its central part. This is one of the steepest gorges reaching the elevation difference of 340 metres in 2.5 kilometres. The path overcoming ladders in long stretches passes by several waterfalls. The three-step Závojový vodopád waterfall with its 65 metres is the tallest in the whole of the Slovenský raj area and the second tallest of Slovakia. The western slopes of the Tomášovská Belá valley are dotted with caves. The lower situated Zlatá diera cave is the subject of interest of speleo-divers. In the past it was frequented by the gold-miners. In 1952 the speleologists (experts on caves) discovered the somewhat higher situated Medvedia jaskyňa cave, with abundant remains of the extinct cave bear *(Ursus spelaeus)*.

In the village of **LETANOVCE** (511 m, population 1,850) with a typical folklore starts the red-marked trial to Kláštorisko. Next to the Letanovský mlyn the path intersects the Prielom Hornádu canyon and ascends the slope

Závojový vodopád waterfall

of the Čertova sihoť Mt. **Kláštorisko** (770 m) the aim of the path is the only tourist centre situated inside the Slovenský raj area accessible only on foot. It is located on a narrow eponymous plateau squeezed between the Prielom Hornádu canyon and the Kyseľ gorge. This situation predetermined Kláštorisko to become a hiding from the enemies for the inhabitants of the area. It served as such also during the Tartar invasion. These events from the past history of Spiš are reflected also in the nomenclatures of the region: Strážny vrch (The Guarding Mountain) or the *Lapis refugii* in Latin meaning the Refuge Rock appearing in the medieval annals from the 13th century. The contemporary name of the place Kláštorisko (The Site of Monastery) is in fact revoking the presence of the Carthusian monks there. Judging from the foundation act from 1299 the Carthusians were granted permission to build a monastery beyond the western wall of the fort where there was also a church. Result of the common efforts of the researchers and conservationists is a remarkable site of the former **Carthusian monastery** amidst the wonderful karstic landscape, in many aspects similar to the romantic ruins of the medieval abbeys for instance in British Isles.

The most interesting access road Kláštorisko comes from the north through the Kláštorská roklina gorge. It is the only one of the two gorges which ends directly in the Prielom Hornádu gorge. The neighbouring Zelená dolina valley with a 25 metres tall waterfall cascade is closed to the public. The Kláštorská roklina gorge was opened to the public only in 1958 when the footbridge over the river Hornád was built. The tallest of the seven waterfalls in the gorge is the Dúhový vodopád waterfall.

On the road connecting Hrabušice with Betlanovce pri Mýte is a turning to the well-known village of **Podlesok** (route No. 7-11), an ideal starting point for the trips to the gorges in the western part of the Slovenský raj and to the upper part of the Prielom Hornádu gorge. Immediately beyond Podlesok the **Suchá Belá** gorge ends in the Hornádska kotlina basin. Its starts on the northern edge of the karstic plateau Glac. It descends by 400 metres in four kilometres.The first complete passage of the gorge was accomplished by a

118

group of young mountaineers lead by A. Mervay in 1910. The tourists could do so only in 1959 after the most beautiful part of the gorge called the Misové vodopády waterfalls with wonderful eddies was made accessible. The name of the waterfall (The Bowl-Like Waterfalls) derives from the fact that the brook disappears in its lower part in a hole, which the experts call ponor, and this is the reason why the bottom under the ponor is usually dry. The tallest of the six waterfalls is the 15 metre tall Okienkový waterfall.

West from Podlesok the river Veľká Biela voda springing on the slope of the Kopanec Mt. (1,132 m) mouths into the Hornád. The Dolina Veľkej Bielej Vody valley is one of the biggest in the Slovenský raj area. It is crossed by the forest road leading to the Dobšinská ľadová jaskyňa ice cave. Two gorges end in the valley. Next to the village Píla the yellow-marked path enters the **Piecky** gorge

Tomášovský výhľad view

ascending to the western edge of the Glac plateau. The whirling water under the waterfalls modelled several rock niches in a form of stove, which gave the name to the gorge (The Little Stoves). The route of ascent branches next to the first waterfall, the marked one is on the left and it is called Stredné Piecky. There are two waterfalls in the Piecky gorge. The 12 metre tall Veľký vodopád waterfall is taller and the other 10 metre tall Terasový vodopád waterfall originated when a ceiling of the cave sank. Thanks to the 300 metre tall cliffs at the Glac plateau the gorge **Veľký Sokol** is quite impressive.

In the place called Kamenná brána the slopes of the gorge leave only a metre wide gap. The end of the gorge is Rothova roklina. In the lower part of Veľký Sokol is another gorge called Malý Sokol which is closed to the public. Before October 5 when the path called **Chodník Horskej služby Prielomom Hornádu** was ceremoniously opened - to the public in summer only the canoeists could enjoy the beauties of the gorge. It is equipped with numerous technical aids making possible easy and comfortable passage over obstacles: 374 metres of chains, 26 metre of ropes, 164 iron steps, 15 iron handles and 85 metres of footbridges secure more than 4 kilometre long route. The sections where the tourists climb the iron steps built-in the rock straight above the water of the Hornád are the most favourite ones. Expo-

Marčeková above Stratená

sure of the stretch in the narrowest part of the gorge called Železná brána squeezed between the almost vertical rock with only 10 metres of space between them makes the tourist stick closer to rock where the iron chain gives them some feeling of safety.

The Slovenský raj Mts. – South

There are several other small mining villages and hamlets scattered amidst beautiful natural setting. Today almost all of them are tourist and recreation villages. Beyond the point, where the valley tapers between Veľká Knola (1,266 m) and Babiná (1,277 m) is the village **MLYNKY** (745 m, population 600, routes No. 23-25) which originated. by joining several hamlets in one. The neighbouring **DEDINKY** (795 m, population 400, routes No. 12-20) on the shore of the water reservoir Palcmanská Maša originated in a similar way.

Dedinky is also a favourite tourist centre open all the year round. In summer it is visited by the water sport fans and hikers. In winter cross-country and down-hill skiing are the sports attracting the visitors. The environs of the village offer outstanding opportunities of hiking on karstic plateaus with superb views of the High Tatras and Kráľova hora Mt. Above the village of Biele Vody there is the only gorge in the southern side of Slovenský raj, Zejrnarská roklina gorge. It was modelled by the water flowing out of the strong karstic spring called Zejmarská studňa. Ascent up the gorge is included in the route of the instructive path Slovenský raj – South which traverses the plateau of Geravy and returns through the opposite lying valley Malé Zajfy back to Dedinky. The humid valley provides ideal conditions for vegetation typical for swamps. The plateau of Geravy is best accessible by a chair lift. High-situated plateau is suitable for cross-country skiing in environment of high-mountain meadows alternating with little forests. The Gačovská skala Mt. (1,099 m) is the place in the south of the plateau offering beautiful views of the Palcmanská Maša dam.

Hnilec from Súľová

Small mountain village **STRATENÁ** (791 m, population 200, routes No. 21, 22) is situated in a wonderful setting of the south-western part of Slovenský raj. In the past the copper, cobalt and nickel ores were mined and processed in local smelting plant. Blast furnaces built here in 1723 belonged to the Coburg company. They were dismantled in 1928. The northern edge of the village is skirted by rocks, part of the southern end of the Lipovec plateau, accessible by green-marked hiking trail, which ends next to **Občasný prameň** spring. West from the Občasný prameň is the **Havrania skala** (1,156 m). If you climb to its top you will get the most impressive views in the Slovak part of the Carpathians.

South from Stratená is the isolated karstic plateau called Pelc. West from Pelc and on the far end of the dolina Tiesňavy valley is the massive mountain of Duča (1,142 m) which enshrines a huge world of caves beneath. The length of discovered corridors in Stratenská jaskyňa cave is now 21,737 metres and the cave is the second longest in Slovakia. It is closed to the public though. Its wonderful dripstone ornamentation including precious aragonite forms and unusually spacious cave corridors and huge halls like Rozprávkový dom (The House of Fairy Tales), the largest underground space in Slovakia with an

Church of Žehra, wall paintings

overall volume of 79,017 cubic metres, 192 metres long, 11 metres high and mean width 46 metres are confined underground and still hidden to the eyes of the public.

Past the village both the road and railway enter the tapered **Stratenská dolina** valley. The valley was created by the upper reach of the river Hnilec, which springs 14 km above, on the slope of the Kráľova hoľa Mt. at elevation of 1,945 m above sea level. The gorge is skirting cliffs in places up to 80 metres high.

The valley widens next to **Dobšinská Ľadová Jaskyňa**, the village, which boasts of the world-famous cave with unique ice filling and ornamentation (routes No. 14, 20). In its space there is 110,132 cubic metres of ice. Its layer is in places more than 25 metres thick! The cave acquired its icy ornamentation because there is only one opening and its shape is that of a bag. It originated some time by the end of the Tertiary era the same as the cave Stratenská from which the Dobšinská cave was separated by a blockage of the communicating corridor. Entrance to the cave is in the highest part of the 80 m deep underground space. In winter cold air enters the cave and pushes the warm air out of its lower parts. In space called The Small Hall the temperature drops to -5° C. The cool air is heavier and it stays in the lower parts of the cave also in summer. As the air circulation is limited the temperature rises only in the upper parts of the cave.

Southern Spiš

Almost the entire south of Spiš spreads in the basin of the Hornád. It is also the lowest situated part of the region so the alternative name the Lower Spiš suits is as well. South of Spiš is separated from Šariš by the Levočské vrchy mountains and the mountain range of Branisko in the north and north-east.

In the centre of the upper part of boasts of Hnilecká dolina valley is the village **NÁLEPKOVO** (538 m, population 2,500, route No. 30). The main road leaves behind the Hnilecká dolina valley in Nálepkovo. It climbs up the val-

The Town Hall of Levoča

ley of Železný potok to small mining village **HNILČÍK** (650 m, population 500), which originated by joining three formerly independent villages (routes No. 27, 28).

The mining village **ŠVEDLÁR** (482 m, population 1,750, route No. 31), founded in the 14th century on the left bank of the river Hnilec is squeezed between two dominating mountains of the Volovské vrchy Mts. In the north it is the Bukovec Mt. (1,227 m) and in the south the mentioned Zlatý stôl Mt. The log roofed bridge over the river Hnilec is from the 19th century. Past the bridge is a typical part of the village that boasts of original miners' houses built in a special architectural style.

KROMPACHY (379 m, population 8,600, routes No. 32, 33, 35) is following Spišská Nová Ves and Levoča the third biggest town of the southern Spiš. Krompachy is a starting point to **Plejsy**, an important ski resort. The ski slopes on the northern side of the Krompašský vrch Mt. (1,025 m) are very popular for their comparatively high standard amenities. Due to its supplies of artificial snow, ski tracks lit in the night and the high capacity of the ski lifts, Plejsy can successfully compete with the best High Tatras ski resorts.

A little trip from Spišská Nová Ves down the stream of the Hornád river is what is needed to visit some remarkable places offering numerous histor-

123

Spišská Kapitula

ical and nature landmarks. **MARKU-ŠOVCE** (445 m, population 2,900) is a village remarkable for its unusual concentration of historical monuments.

A pleasant walk around the village can refresh the visit to Markušovce (route No. 36). The yellow-marked footpath leads from the village to the **stone mushroom of Markušovce**, a protected nature phenomenon in the neighbouring village Matejovce.

Since ancient times the heart of the Spiš region was the eastern edge of the Hornádska kotlina basin. The land was ruled from behind the walls of Spiš Castle by the heads of the region and the ecclesiastical life was organised in Spišská Kapitula (the Spiš Canonry) by the bishops, provosts, and canonists. In a valley between these two centres of power the small town of **SPIŠSKÉ PODHRADIE** (435 m, population 3,500) originated. The eastern horizon of Spišské Podhradie is occupied by the Spiš Castle standing on the land administered by the community of Žehra situated at the opposite side of the hill. As a national cultural monument **Spiš Castle**, with its area of more than 4 ha, and partially in ruins, is one of the largest castle compounds in Central Europe.

The landscape around the community of Spišské Podhradie can be seen comfortably by using the tourist educational footpath Sivá Brada-Dreveník (route No. 37), which has seven information boards along its route informing the visitor about the seven travertine hills and the significant natural phenomenon of this part of the region. Its length is 14.5 km. The footpath starts at the mineral water spring in Sivá Brada, where drivers travelling by car along the main road from Poprad to Prešov frequently prefer to stop. At the top of a low travertine hill stands pilgrim's chapel of 1675. The hill is a fine example of a still "living" (in terminology of geologists) originating travertine form and has been a nature reserve from 1979.

The city of **LEVOČA** (573 m, population 13,800, routes No. 38, 39, 40) is often considered the brightest jewel in the Spiš crown. It lies near the northern edge of the Hornádska kotlina basin at the southern foothills of the Levočské vrchy mountains. High above the town towers the **Mariánska hora** mountain (760 m). It is the biggest meeting point of pilgrims in Slovakia. Thousands of worshippers climb the mountain in long queues to express their gratitude to the Virgin Mary at the Neo-Gothic church of Visitation of the Virgin Mary from the early 20th century.

Register (The entries are followed by numbers of routes)